Selling Sex
in *Utah*

Selling Sex in Utah

A HISTORY OF VICE

Eileen Hallet Stone

THE
History
PRESS

Published by The History Press
Charleston, SC
www.historypress.com

First published 2023

Manufactured in the United States

ISBN 9781467149112

Library of Congress Control Number: 2022951606

CONTENTS

PREFACE

What's in a name?

A rose is a rose is a rose.
It is what it is what it is. It's straightforward.

But the name-calling of prostitutes is abundant…

abandoned woman	harlot
bar girl	hog
bawd	hooker
bird	hussy
bird of paradise	hustler
boarder	inmate
camp follower	inmate of the roost
cat	lady of easy virtue
crib girl	lady of the night
daughter of Venus	minx
daughter of joy	nymph du pave
demi-monde	of the calling
erring sister	old-timer
fallen angel	painted lady
fallen woman	prairie nymph
fille de joie	pretty waiter girl
fledging	prostitute

C.E. Johnson, *Modesty*, 1904. *Photograph courtesy of the Special Collections, Merrill-Cazier Library, Utah State University.*

pullet
scarlet lady
seamstress
sex worker
soiled dove
sporting girl
streetwalker

strumpet
temptress
tramp
upstairs girl
wayward sister
whore
working girl

…and, in Utah, complicated.

ACKNOWLEDGEMENTS

I began researching material for this book around the beginning of the COVID pandemic, and by its end—if indeed there is an end—it harmed countless numbers of people and took the lives of some six hundred thousand people in the United States. Schools, colleges, public entities, libraries, businesses, stores, shops and restaurants—nearly everything—closed. People like my husband and me self-isolated, worked from home, wore masks in public and, thankfully, waited it out.

But with the closures of museums, university special collections, archives, research centers, I am grateful to have received immense help from so many people who were also at home, self-isolating and making it through.

To Elizabeth Rogers, curator of manuscripts at the University of Utah Marriott Library, Salt Lake City, Utah; Sara Davis, senior photograph archivist; Lorraine Crouse, senior photograph archivist (retired); and Molly Steed, head of multimedia archives and curator of multimedia, I am indebted to you for your advice, patience and wonderful images.

I am grateful to Doug Misner, research/collections manager at Utah State History in Salt Lake City. I applaud his action in caring for glass plate negatives and in persisting to obtain extensive high-resolution images for this book, all the while moving the entire state history collection from the damaged Rio Grande Depot to temporary quarters as a result of the Tooele earthquake three years ago.

I am thankful for Daniel Davis, photograph curator at the Merrill-Cazier Library, Utah State University, in Logan, Utah, for allowing me use of the

Charles Ellis Johnson photographs from the library's collection and for contributing to this book's content with his insight and words.

With fond appreciation, I thank Elaine Carr of the Regional History Center at Uintah County Library in Vernal, Utah, who always and kindly comes through with the rare photograph I need.

I appreciate all the comments and images given to me by Roman Vega, the director of the Western Mining Railroad Museum in Helper, Utah.

I value the help with images and Ogden insights given to me by Sara Langsdon, the head of special collections at Stewart Library, Weber State University, in Ogden, Utah. I am also grateful to Morgan Pierce, the executive director of the Park City Museum in Park City, Utah, for his help in obtaining photographs of the city's old red-light district.

I thank Elaine Thornton, assistant director of the History of Health Sciences, Spencer S. Eccles Health Sciences Library, University of Utah Marriott Library, in Salt Lake City, Utah, for researching medical issues for me and allowing my husband, Randy, to set up and photograph patent medicines for this book. I also want to thank Steven Greenburg, the coordinator of public services (retired) at the National Library of Medicine's History of Medicine Division in Washington, D.C., who helped me better understand sexually transmitted diseases and their effects on the early frontier prostitutes.

I owe much to Valerie Jacobson and Heidi Stringham at the Utah Division of State Archives and Records Service (Research Center) in Salt Lake for their commitment in finding two obscure trial cases that took me into the lives of my subjects.

Special thanks to Tina Kirkham, the digital library project manager at the University of Utah Marriott Library, who helped me delve deeper into the digital newspaper archives to find a treasure trove of essential and supportive information. I also want to thank Ken Rockwell, the intrepid map librarian at the Marriot Library, for his details of the borders that existed or didn't in the Territory of Utah.

I am appreciative of Tom Carter, professor of architectural history (emeritus) at the University of Utah, College of Architecture and Planning, for taking the time to explain the architecture of Ogden's Twenty-Fifth Street and the resultant and wild Electric Alley.

Thanks to historian and author Dr. Steven Lacy of Murray, Utah, for his contribution of images and content to my book. Thanks also to documentary filmmaker and photographer Diane Orr, Salt Lake City and singer and acoustic guitar player Paul Rasmussen and Cassie Leconte, all of whom opened my research quest to further exploration and offered great contacts and information.

I value Morgan Browning, head of paper conservation at the National Archives and Records Administration in Washington, D.C., for his insight and newspaper accounts of his illustrious relative in Ogden. I also want to thank former Ogdenite Robin Macnofsky for her knowledgeable revelation on Ogden's Twenty-Fifth Street and its tunnels.

I take my hat off to Artie Crisp, senior acquisition editor at The History Press, for his patience during these tenuous times; to copy editor Ashley Hill for making sense of and improving my style of writing; and to cover designer Caroline Rodrigues for their instrumental help in bringing this book to its wide-ranging fruition.

To my son, Daniel, and his lovely wife, Stephanie, thank you for your enthusiasm during the long process of researching and writing this book. To my husband, Randy Silverman, thank you for your wholehearted support, humor, thoughtful caring and the willingness to stop on a dime for every extraordinary and ordinary story that appeared in the offing. And to the remarkable Dr. Wallace L. Akerley, the incredible mensch and healer at Huntsman Cancer Institute at the Circle of Hope Drive in Salt Lake City, thank you.

I apologize for whatever mistakes of omission may have occurred.

INTRODUCTION

A profession both blatant and hidden in our society, prostitution was treading the boards of the Victorian era in which gender was "biologically based" on the centuries-old, double-standard premise that men and women embody opposite orbs that, in traditional form and function, define their sex. Generally, men wanted and needed sex, but women were not so disposed, except to please their husbands. Men were strong; women were weak. Men were independent and public; women were dependent and cloistered. Men received pay for their work; women who were tending to children and hearth did not. Sex was not discussed. Men could risk abandoning the home. Wives could become destitute. Egalitarianism was rarely a given.

Maybe it was truly a matter of class—the upper (elite wealthy) and middle (educated) classes maintained by the sanctity of reputation, privilege and money—that buttressed the peculiar and nonetheless traditional distinction that triggered bedlam along the mostly—but not limited to—lower class. Prostitution was a moral menace, and for some a financial obligation.

Where did the abandoned women lacking funds go? What option did these girls have after being thrown out of their houses by parents appalled by their daughters' reputation and fearful that it would disgrace their standing? What happened to the children who were put to the streets by their fathers to sell sex—or their deserted mothers whose only income was gained through prostitution? Where did one go after being sexually molested and abused by a family member? Why prostitution?

C.E. Johnson, *Flirting. Photograph courtesy of the Special Collections, Merrill-Cazier Library, Utah State University.*

LISTENING FOR STORIES

Years back, writing articles for a fine magazine called *Network*, I was handed an index card scribbled with Utah addresses of possible prostitutes.

Going by car with a cop friend into the vast and empty parking lot behind a closed giant of a department store that began its retail merchandise business with a mail-order catalogue in 1863, I watched as women solicited on the street, tempting punters with their looks (cosmetic and provocative), clothes (half-zipped jeans and tight tops) and hard-to-decipher attitudes that shifted from annoyance to enticement with each successive interaction.

A few days later, I attempted to interview truckdrivers in oversized rigs idling on a spot near the city's railroad tracks and was soon penned in on both sides of my car until I promised to turn off my tape recorder. Even then, embarrassment was followed by anger, and they took off. Did I say the parking lot was dusty?

I watched a woman work a man who was sitting at a hotel bar downtown. She was stunning but not, as a call girl told me, on easy street. Treating a working woman to breakfast at a local pancake house in exchange for an interview, she left to wash up, and the coffee got cold. On State Street, I saw women handing cash over to men who were standing outside a motel when my car parked across the street died. Sneaking out to find the nearest telephone booth, I called my brother Michael and waited for an hour or so until he picked me up and got the car towed. He suggested that there were other ways to research; I would have loved a new car.

I picked up information. But it was the time I spent on a side street on the west side of town that showed me I would have to learn to listen beyond the words.

Following a series of garages containing miscellaneous stalls, repair shops, secondhand stores and several Saran-wrapped boats and trailers was an open gate in a white picket fence leading to a small house in need of paint. Walking up the path, I barely touched the doorbell when two Great Danes with massive heads lumbered out. (I'm from Maine and don't like to acknowledge fear.) Within seconds, shooing away the magnificent beasts, a young man invited me inside, where he said his boss was in the studio auditioning a young woman on a pole. The music was loud. The dance floor gleamed. Its ceiling was wrapped in mirrors. A girl in a T-shirt and shorts struggled through a pole dance routine. The "boss" looked patient, but the air hung low without much promise. I had the idea it might have been his sister's daughter in need of a job.

In the kitchen, four or five women were sitting around a table, drinking coffee. They talked about becoming prostitutes. Some mentioned abuse; running from home; escaping from a boyfriend or a violent madam; keeping the undergarments of the Mormon men they served; and never kissing a customer on the lips. They talked a lot, sometimes simultaneously, and they laughed a lot. There was no need for questions. They had a script, and I had been played. It wasn't until listening to their gestures and posturing, how they leaned into one another and how their eyes kept saying something different, that I finally heard: "A rose is a rose is a rose." What is, is what is, is what is. Listening to their body language while having another cup of coffee, the litany of words faded to essences, and I found my story.

ENQUIRY

After Artie Crisp, the senior acquisition editor at The History Press, sent me a list of topics, offering the opportunity of choice, I was in, and *Selling Sex in Utah: A History of Vice* was a go.

Although prostitution in this state seemed like a shadow of what was blatantly occurring in most other states, fading into the underpinnings of obscurity in Utah, research was key to gleaning the significance of prostitution in this state—from the frontier days in the Old West, when the Territory of Utah was dramatically vast, to the illegal red-light districts that emerged in many of the state's cities, towns, rural boroughs and mining and railroad sites and were woven into the very fabric of this state's history.

I strove for stories, real accounts, about Utah's prostitutes that reflected individual humanity, including the trials and tribulations in their lives—stories that uncover men who were romantically drawn to soiled doves or were taken by female hustlers, such as the chronicle of Judge Drummond's lapse in judgement. I was also intrigued by stories of madams with entrepreneurial prowess, like Belle London, whose proclivity to make money stunned the city's male businessmen, and Kate Flint, whose resistance to a court ruling that smeared her character would not be taken lying down.

Culling through archived newspaper accounts, readings, interviews and personal court trials, I discovered independent subcultures that flourished in the red-light districts of the past. An array of lifestyles came alive with challenges that flew in the face of overwhelming odds: quarreling bar girls; controlling lovers; aggressive customers; the promiscuity of painted ladies and the brutality and the health risks from which pretty waiter girls, streetwalkers and brothel inmates endured or died; the impermanence and frailty of such work; the symbiotic and aggrieved relationship with city officials, commissioners, police, sheriffs, judges and city council members that may have benefitted from a constant source of fines; and numbers of legal businessmen and individuals who opted to make public and private but thoroughly illegal profits, as shown in the construction of a large stockade and the decision to corral women in Salt Lake City.

The exclusivity of Utah was problematic, and early on, newspaper articles waged the Mormon/gentile (non-Mormon) conflict, resulting in intense distrust, and strident clashes on issues of prostitution. The dominant religious society led by the Church of Jesus Christ of Latter-day Saints was long in battle over polygamy, which they considered their spiritual right and which kept Utah from receiving statehood until they acquiesced. Mormons shunned the depravity displayed by public women (prostitutes), who they believed were brought into the state by gentiles. And yet, despite numerous raids and campaigns deployed against prostitution, the Mormons tolerated its existence. Although common ground could be found among Mormons and gentiles, it would take some time for it to be found.

Charles Ellis Johnson's erotic stereographic images are interleaved throughout this book. Reflecting the LDS photographer's scandalous sideline from the 1890s into the 1900s, they would have shocked many Latter-day Saints and been solidly denounced as indecent by LDS church officials. Although "dubious in plot," these risqué images are replete with "sexual overtones" and extend the historical content of our complicated gender, class and sexual trends.

The resultant stories are full, many and varied—and in their humanness, alive.

1

EROTICA

Rules of Behavior

Utah's early theaters were the embodiment of spectacles, performances, plays, dramas, minstrels, soliloquys, opera, stage settings, lighting and costumes. They were also a mix of cultural and historical bits that temporarily took people out of their day-to-day surroundings and work environment into experiences filled with emotions, perceptions, attractions and, most of all, entertainment.

Brigham Young, the second president of the Church of Jesus Christ of Latter-day Saints and Utah's territorial governor from 1850 to 1857, maintained that living in remote isolation from the rest of the country, "the people must have amusement as well as religion."[1]

With posters reflecting rules of behavior for both actors and the audience—in Corrine, Utah's opera house, there were catcalls, yelling, whispering, a little bit of drunkenness, romantic liaisons and even a stomping of heavy boots, but only one dogfight ever took place—several theaters opened, aspiring to deliver uplifting amusement and "wholesome, innocent drama."

Under the direction of President Brigham Young, the exquisite, multitiered Salt Lake Theater, built at a cost of over $100,000, debuted in 1861 on the northwest corner of State Street and First South Street to an enthusiastic audience of 1,200.

According to former professors of church history at Brigham Young University Kenneth L. Alford and Robert C. Freeman:

The first time Brigham Young imposed any censorship on the theatre was during the first professional ballet to appear in it. Young instructed the manager that all ballet skirts must be ankle length. The manager protested that it would be impossible for the troupe to dance, but Young was insistent.

During the first performance, many of the dancers tripped and fell [over their] long skirts. Before the second performance, the manager cut one inch off the skirts. When this went unnoticed by Young, the manager cut off another inch at the next performance and continued doing this until, by the final night of the ballet, the skirts had been shortened to their original length. Brigham Young had attended every performance and either hadn't noticed or pretended he hadn't![2]

Over the years, controlling content, the audience and legions of actors, dancers and burlesque chorus lines arriving in Utah on their way to California was near impossible, a gamble at best that proved unprofitable. In 1911, LDS president Joseph F. Smith did not mince words:

We have some interest in the old Salt Lake Theater…but when we get high-class performances in that theatre, the benches are practically empty, while the vaudeville theatres, where there are exhibitions of nakedness, of obscenity, of vulgarity, and everything else that does not tend to elevate the thought and mind of man, will be packed from pit to dome.…I wish to say to the Latter-day Saints that I hope they will distinguish themselves by avoiding the necessity of being classed with people who prefer the vulgar to the chaste, the obscene to the pure, the evil to the good, and the sensual to the intellectual.[3]

An Eagerness to Be

The famed Salt Lake City photographer Charles Ellis Johnson was born in 1857 to Latter-day Saint parents, Joseph Johnson and his third wife, Eliza Saunders, although for several years, few knew about this new wife, mother and child.

Joseph was the son of Mormons who were esteemed (often referred to as the "royal family") for being among the first families to participate in religious leader and founder of the Mormon faith Joseph Smith's "'new and eternal covenant' of polygamous marriage."[4]

Independent and innovative, Joseph evolved into a man of many skills; he was a schoolteacher, arborist/horticulturist, shopkeeper, manufacturer of

C.E. Johnson, *In the Shadow of the LDS Temple. Photograph courtesy of the Special Collections, Merrill-Cazier Library, Utah State University.*

homemade medical remedies, postman and a newspaper editor who smoked cigars and sold "spiritous liquors."

Already engaged in a plural marriage with two wives, Joseph and his family moved to several states and, for numerous reasons, were not keen to relocate to Utah. His marriage to a much younger sixteen-year-old (he was nearly forty) was kept secret from his other wives. The bride, Eliza, continued to live in her parents' house, and they were adamantly opposed to plural marriages. The boy, Charles, called his mother Liza. Joseph faced charges in Iowa, and only with help from non-Mormon friends and business contacts was he able to extricate himself from the sway of the law. But the family did move to Salt Lake City and, directed by Brigham Young, went to St. George, where through trial and error, Joseph made portions of the dry desert bloom with fruit trees, vegetables, honeysuckle, flowering almonds, John Hopper perpetual roses, transplanted trees and magnificently lush flowers.

Charles grew up in a home that honored culture and scholarship. He developed an insatiable curiosity and was intrigued with anthropology, botany, mechanical inventions and modern technology. He devoured

C.E. Johnson,
*Rose. Photograph
courtesy of the Special
Collections, Merrill-
Cazier Library, Utah
State University.*

literature, history and the arts—all leading to his love affair with all theaters, both on stage and off—travel and photography.

By 1890, Charles Ellis Johnson was an unofficial photographer for the LDS Church and a self-styled photojournalist, and advertising "You'll See Johnson All Over the World," a consummate if clandestine photographer and stereographer of erotica.

In "Appreciating a Pretty Shoulder: The Risquie Images of Charles Ellis Johnson," Daniel Davis, a photograph curator at Utah State University in Logan, which houses a fascinating collection of Johnson's erotica, wrote, "Charles made images of attractive women a specialty…reflecting the general trends toward greater nudity and a more voyeuristic depiction of women for the 1890s to the early 1900s."[5]

There were a lot of surprises vis-à-vis Johnson. A tall, handsome and genteel man who most likely acquired his refined countenance from his London-born mother (said to have been the illegitimate daughter of an

English aristocrat), Johnson photographed hundreds of native and touring thespians, burlesque dancers and musical vaudeville cabarets.

Working as an actor while in St. George, Johnson managed a small theater and wrote weekly columns for the *New York Dramatic Mirror*, founded in 1879. When he was older and living in Salt Lake City, he built his own cameras and, as a distributor for American Stars bicycles, would grab his preferred camera equipment, jump on his American Star and capture on-glass images of Salt Lake locales, Latter-day Saint apostles, attractive women and every other image he thought worth capturing. This included memorializing the incumbent President Teddy Roosevelt, who, during a fourteen-thousand-mile tour of the West, stopped by his host, Utah senator and mining magnate Thomas Kearns's mansion in Salt Lake City in 1903.

Perhaps picking up cues from his father, for whom he often wrote newspaper articles and worked in his stores, Charles also manufactured and sold patent medicines under his label, Valley Tan Remedies (VTR). He co-owned a pharmacy business with Parley P. Pratt, the son of Quorum of the Twelve Apostles Parley Parker Pratt, who was killed by the estranged husband of the woman who had become the Apostle's twelfth wife. Working as a business manager in Hyrum Sainsbury's photography studio, he became drawn to the photographic process. When Sainsbury retired during the 1893 national depression, Charles and Parley bought him out.

Often photographing his subjects in the studio's back room, where background scenes, costumes and lighting were dramatic and accessible, Charles sold his work in various formats. Priced to appeal to an assortment of customers, it ranged from photographer-signed and noted stereo views, postcards and prints for Salt Lake newspapers to the small carte-de-visité visiting cards and the larger four-and-a-half-by-six-and-a-half-inch cabinet cards, all usually mounted on stiff cardboard embellished with his studio's identifiers. Those that featured scandalous burlesque women in various stages of undress and inuendo were quickly swept up.

Insatiable, Charles acquired a printing press, designed and printed his own stationary and, when necessary, wrapped erotic photography purchases in plain paper for customers departing the studio. Tracing tourist pilgrimages throughout the city and around the splendid Latter-day Saint temple, Charles opened a giftshop lined with postcards dedicated to LDS monuments, buildings, churches, church officials, conferences and dedications. He waded into the then rare mail-order business, selling his photographs across state lines and oceans. It's a wonder he wasn't caught mailing images that were considered obscene and illegal in that day.

Self-made and motivated, Charles was not without tumult. While living in St. George, he met and fell in love with Ruth Young, one of Brigham Young's daughters. According to Mary Campbell's *Charles Ellis Johnson and the Erotic Mormon Image*, President Brigham Young and several family members wintered in their St. George home, which was located directly behind Joseph Johnson's house and his magnificent flower and rose gardens, through which the venerable LDS leader liked to stroll.[6] "[Charles] met Ruth, or Ruthie, as everyone called her, at a party in St. George," Campbell wrote. "[M]arried in the St. George Temple in 1878, within five years, they had two sons and were living in Salt Lake City. Like her husband, Ruthie had a taste for the fashionable and the new."[7]

An almost picture-perfect couple, their union did not last. Taking sons Ellis and Jay Elliot with her, Ruth left Charles. Though devastated, Charles begged her to return; she didn't and apparently went to California. Little is known about her reasoning, but family lore suggests she had an affair. In 1887, the abandoned husband filed for divorce. Propped up by both the Young and Johnson families, LeGrand Young (Ruth's cousin) represented him in the divorce proceedings. Ellis and Jay Elliot did return to Utah. Out of favor and out of state, Ruth eventually converted to Methodism.

Charles built portfolios of images taken at the dedication of Salt Lake City's temple, the 1893 Chicago World's Fair with the Mormon Tabernacle Choir and then on to San Francisco in 1896. Davis wrote the photographer "shot group portraits of the first presidency and the quorum of the twelve and sold reprints of older Brigham Young photographs."[8]

In the late 1890s, Johnson also published stereographic sequences that, viewed chronologically, tell a visual story, sometimes dubious in plot but replete with "sexual overtones." At the turn of the century, he became more brazen and began showing more bareness in his stereocards of partially nude women baring garters, stockings, uncovered shoulders, thighs, "semi-transparent clothing" and half-exposed breasts.

Likely the only Mormon photographer in Utah at the time to capture thousands of risqué images, Johnson walked a fine line between his religious association with the LDS Church and his lifelong, incredibly seductive avocation.

Surely, if church officials—especially those who had their portraits taken in his studio—knew of his scandalous sideline, they would have condemned his illicit work. It is puzzling that they didn't know—or just kept silent.

Perhaps Charles, a thoughtful and considerate individual who, when he was twenty-four years old, took care of his siblings after their father's death and later employed them to work in his shop, would not want to inflict any heartache on his extended family or impart a stain on their reputation. It's possible that traveling overseas and soaking in the customs, traditions, exotic dances, "orientalism" and theatrical climes in other cultures, he was able to tactfully step sideways from church participation and, as his father did and so advised, maintained a respectful, casual association. It's also conceivable that Charles loved and needed to picture life in all its outstanding facets. Then, of course, it could be that business is business and he knew to keep his moneymaker discreet.

Daniel Davis writes that Johnson did not journal his personal thoughts—in fact, he left very little writing behind. But around 1903–4, we learn Charles left his siblings in charge of his businesses and spent almost a year in the Holy Land, taking more than two thousand photographs with Madame Lydia Mary Olive (Mamreoff von Finkelstein) Mountford. The woman was a missionary, journalist and actress who staged biblical plays. Born in Jerusalem to Russian Jewish parents who converted to nonsectarian Christianity, she later became a Mormon and married Wilford Woodruff, a later LDS president.

While Charles was away, his brothers, struggling to keep up, hired Minnie B. Ridley to help manage the businesses. Rushing home to rescue the boys, Charles discovered the Ridley woman to be phenomenally efficient. The two straightened out the shops, the brothers were given the VTR pharmacy and, for nearly ten years, the couple worked well together.

Some unconfirmed opinions implied they were lovers. "In 1914, Miss Ridley died, and Charles sold his businesses," Davis wrote. "In 1916, he moved to San Jose, California, to live with the Ridley family…who were [non-LDS] and nearly strangers."[9]

According to Campbell, although Charles and Minnie never married, they lived together in the shop. He signed her death certificate (she was forty-eight years old), and after moving to San Jose, he opened another successful shop. He seemed happy.

Making plans to visit kin back in Utah, Charles died of heart failure in 1926 and, with a Christian minister officiating, was buried in San Jose's Oak Hill Cemetery.

2

TERRITORY, FRONTIER PROSTITUTES, DISEASES, POISONOUS CURES

*L*ong before the 1820s, trappers, traders, mountain men and rugged hide hunters roamed America's remote western wilderness for beaver pelts, chasing the aquatic animal to near extinction before turning to buffalo robes and selling them in the American and Canadian fur trade. In far-flung areas, many former trappers set up trading posts and built forts along key trade routes—perhaps the few places where independent and weathered men might congregate.

It was a booming if not lonely business until the profitable beaver and hide trade waned and the emigrant routes and trails were taken up by a new population in the nation's western expansion. By the 1850s, the river towns of Kansas City and St. Joseph along the long Missouri River stood out among the "jumping off points," considered the first leg toward the western frontier for voyagers, prospectors and pioneers.

Beyond What the Eye Can See: 1850 Territory of Utah

For thousands of years, much of the massive and complicated topography of Utah comprised mountains, canyons, deserts, arroyos. And the prairies in America's western regions had been inhabited by the indigenous first people, such as the ancient Puebloans, Navajo, Ute, Paiute and Goshute.

As early as 1540, the enormity of the western wilderness, its potential for colonization and religious conversion and Spain's vigorous El Dorado–fixated pursuit of precious metal riches and wealth pushed vanquishers like Commander Garca-López de Cárdenas y Figueroa to lead one of the first recorded Spanish expeditions along Mexico's western coast and into what is now the southwestern United States and, most likely, Utah.

In 1598, Spanish conquistador Juan de Oñate y Salazar, the son of a wealthy silver mine owner, along with some four hundred men (settlers) and seven thousand head of stock, went to claim and colonize New Mexico for Spain.

Former University of Utah professor William H. Gonzalez and diversity pioneer and former University of Utah associate vice-president of academic affairs Orlando Rivera explained in the online article "Hispanics of Utah" for the *Utah History Encyclopedia* that the Spaniards set up "their headquarters across from the Indian pueblo of San Juan near present-day Espanola."[10]

In 1609, Spanish official Pedro de Peralta, the then-appointed governor of New Mexico (1610–13), founded New Mexico's capital city of Santa Fe when it was a province of New Spain. "Once this was done, Spanish colonization spread throughout the area," the historians wrote.

For more than two hundred years, the Spanish flag flew over the city until 1822, when it was supplanted by the Mexican flag. People's lifestyles remained pretty much the same. But after declaring war on Mexico in 1846, the United States invaded the nation. Two years later, the Treaty of Guadalupe Hidalgo (considered a treaty of "peace and friendship") was signed between the two countries, and the United States took possession of much of northern Mexico, including present-day Utah.

According to the contract, the two historians penned, "the inhabitants of the north, who, for centuries, had resided in the area, remained there with their rights to property and the freedom to communicate in Spanish ostensibly granted them"—but not for long. "Under the new government [and] having to pay taxes on their land few could afford, they soon lost most of their land, their water rights, their freedom of expression, and did not truly share in a representative government. These events resulted in poverty, forcing them to move from the lands of their ancestors to places where they could find employment [so they could] survive."

After an arduous 111-day journey, in 1847, the first group of pioneering Mormons seeking political and religious freedom arrived in Salt Lake Valley (Utah), which was then a part of Mexico. With the establishment of Salt Lake City and some smaller settlement towns in the north, the early settlers, under the leadership of Brigham Young, petitioned Congress for entry into the Union as the State of Deseret, including Salt Lake City as its capital and all the borders that encompassed the extensive wilderness, much of it comprising the nation's current western states.

At the time, there were no designated borders defining the western landscape. In a personal email, Ken Rockwell, the map librarian at the University of Utah's Marriott Library, clarified that official boundaries didn't exist "until 1850, when the federal government established the Territory of Utah."[11]

"The incorporated Territory of Utah," he explained, "contained present-day Utah, following the north and south boundaries with the same latitudes as today (37 to 48 degrees north). But the territory extended west to the boundary of the new State of California (thus encompassing most of today's Nevada) and eastward to the spine of the Rockies (then not too well surveyed) to take in western Colorado and southwestern Wyoming."

For the deluge of controversial issues that erupted, were talked about, thrashed out, argued, debated and disputed, it would take about forty-six years for the feisty and independent territory, with its shrinking borders and requirements outlined by Congress—specifically, relinquishing polygamy—to join the Union as the State of Utah.

In the Thick of It

The Wild West was as staggeringly enormous as its medicine was woefully primitive. Life expectancy was short. Doctors, mostly trained as surgeons, were few and far between.[12] The consequences of medical mishaps in remote areas on rough trails could turn calamitous. Treatments for those suffering from bullet wounds; injuries acquired in Indian raids, animal attacks, brawls, feuds; broken bones; scurvy; infections; dysentery; and any other number of physical or emotional ailments, illnesses or sicknesses relied more on personal knowledge, home or folk remedies and almanacs like the *Old Farmer's Almanac*, first published in 1818.

And yet, wherever hordes of men traveled west, hoping to discover riches, prostitutes were sure to follow. Most of these young girls and women were down to their last dime. Some had been orphaned as children, while others came from turbulent broken homes, were turned away by their families, were sexually violated by family members, were compelled (or sold) into the prostitution trade by impoverished parents or were fleeing vicious past

C.E. Johnson, *Tired. Photograph courtesy of the Special Collections, Merrill-Cazier Library, Utah State University.*

traumas. There were widows without recourse and wives who had been divorced, abandoned or deserted by husbands without proper recompense. With no safety net and unable to find gainful employment, their survival was grim with respite, so they were told, in the less-exploited West.

Then there were others, mostly young and energetic, who gamely chanced the profession as a new and exciting adventure: dancing, drinking, entertaining, flirting and evocatively seizing all manner of men. Markedly, most of their undertakings centered on the business of making money by selling sex. The untamed western frontier beamed untold opportunity—or so it was believed. Maybe they could even find husbands, get out of the trade and gain sought-after respectability.

Working girls arrived in the West alone, in groups and in clusters, recruited by formerly urban madams, spellbound by weathercocks, seduced by opportunists, the result of being trafficked or just driven by hope or desperation. They were mostly white women, some as young as fourteen. They chased independent gold diggers and prospectors who were ravenous for female contact and willing to pay for sexual trysts off any trail and in any covered wagon. Prostitutes set up tents near early mining's narrow-gauge railroad tracks. They plied their trade in rough shanties, conducted business on blankets under trees (hence the name "blanket whore") and carried out hazard side-work in hastily assembled, hard-pressed, hard-hitting bars. In early established mining communities, they attached themselves to madam-run stables in primarily male-owned saloons that were reputed to be the rowdy "heartbeat of the frontier," where men gathered to drink, get drunk, conduct business, review the news, gamble, fight, socialize and, with any luck—and money left over—get with a girl, any girl.

In this new, raw environment dominated by men, many with lawless self-interest and behaviors that swung from sanguine to aggression, these working girls also became easy victims of intimidation, abuse, rape—about which they kept to themselves (Who would believe them anyway?)—and murder.

It is true that among the many types of women who worked in saloons and dancehalls, there were those fallen doves who treated customers of all mindsets with nonconfrontational, pleasant dispositions, and there were others who were predisposed to the forceful milieu and relentless sexual activity widely inherent in the male-saturated frontier camps.

Who knows what anyone was thinking; but either way, it was no easy role to play. Those new to the sex business contended with personal miseries over which they had little or no control and tempered their frailty with drugs, alcohol and addiction. However one reasoned her future, one thing was clear: being sexually active with multiple customers meant she gambled her life with exposure to venereal diseases and the virulent syphilis, the bacterial infection for which there was no existing medical treatment or cure.

THE VENEREAL DISEASE, SYPHILIS

The term *venereal*, derived from the word *venery*, refers to Venus, the Roman goddess of love, beauty, sexuality and persuasion. Syphilis, caused by the

Girolamo, *Predica Dellarte de Bene Morrie* (Florence, Bartolommeo di Libra, after November 2, 1496). *Photograph courtesy of the Library of Congress.*

bacterium *Treponema pallidum*, was introduced in a 1530 poem by poet, scholar and physician Girolamo Fracastoro. Titled *Syphilis, Sive Morbus Gallicus* (the French disease), the poem follows the story of Syphilis, a mythological shepherd, who is tending to King Alcathous's flock. Syphilis became angry when a drought affected his people. He cursed and blamed the sun god for the drought, so the sun god meted out punishment to the shepherd and his people with a repugnant and smelly new disease. Also known as the great pox (and, in the West, "the clap," "calamity" and "gambler's rot"), syphilis was recognized as dangerous and lethal.

Syphilis was identified in Italy several years after Italian explorer and navigator Christopher Columbus (Cristoforo Colombo) returned from his sea voyage to the new world in 1493. His crew of seamen were possibly infected after having sexual intercourse with women wherever they dropped anchor, such as in the coastal island of Hispaniola in the Caribbean.

As to who gave syphilis to whom, some views suggest the disease was already present in both Europe and everywhere else in the world long before Columbus's new world voyage.[13] According to Vern L. Bullough in *The History of Prostitution*, the disease, called morbus gallicus (the French disease), was observed among "the soldiers of the French army garrisoning Naples in 1495."[14] This is no reflection on France, as nearly every culture and country was blamed for infecting another population.

STEALTH MOVES

Syphilis travels predominantly from one person to another person through sexual intercourse. After an incubation period of ten to ninety days—when an infected transmitter's identity, especially if there were no signs of the disease, would be obfuscated for those prostitutes who were servicing streams of men—the first phase of syphilis appears as chancre, painless ulcers that transmit the disease and are commonly seen on genitals that, within weeks, recede, leaving a slight visible scar.

In *Women and Prostitution: A Social History*, authors Vern Bullough and Bonnie Bullough explain the second phase of the disease, which emerges four to eight weeks later, with patients experiencing various reactions from "skin rashes, sores in the mouth" to "sporadic fevers and headaches, sore throat" and ulcers that appear on other parts of the body.[15]

Although these symptoms also diminish over time, the disease does not. In the disease's third, latent phase, the infected person becomes highly contagious for several years. Then, if they are not dead from other causes, the disease will erupt into the last phase that, left untreated, will ravage the body and mind with severe and advanced lesions (called "gumma") on the skin and in bones and vital organs, such as the heart and brain. And finally, the disease attacks "the nervous system [and] causes paralysis and insanity," leading to the frequently inevitable final phase: death.

Hygiene

An experienced madam setting up a sex business on the western frontier would know the consequences of venereal disease. She was the closest thing to a medical reference those under her oversight had. She often had recommended health measures for both feminine and social hygiene and cleanliness and forms of fumigation (disinfectant).

Of course, such preventive remedies that required fresh, clean water might not have been easily employed. Unless one lived by a stream, bathing took place weekly. Water basins were reused, and according to Kistrin Holt's "Soap Making on the Old West Homestead," soaps were made from boiled "animal fat, wood ashes, and water," involving a long, smelly process that was more often done outdoors.[16] Blends of soap, chalk and charcoal were used to make early forms of toothpaste, which tasted like soap. Until the mid-1880s, perfume was the deodorant of choice.

With little grasp of syphilis's gravity, the importance of hygiene was not likely fully understood by frontier prostitutes. Left untreated, the infectious disease could spread from one person to another—prostitute and patron—creating an ill-omened and pernicious cycle, especially when serving multiple partners at a commercial pace. Inspecting and washing each client's genitals with soap, fresh water and an antiseptic solution before having sexual relations was considered time-consuming and troublesome.

According to Jeremy Agnew in his book *Brides of the Multitude*, douches containing such antiseptic solutions as mercury, water-soluble mercuric cyanide and carbolic acid caused discomfort and were often too harsh and inconvenient for women to use.[17]

Pregnancy was problematic for most prostitutes, and unless they had an empathetic madam, it could cost them their career. Among "fallen angels" working in the West, despite the risks to their life and health, abortions were often chosen over the use of contraceptives. In *Red Light Women of the Rocky Mountains*, historian Jan MacKell recorded frontier methods of abortion

Imported from Europe, condoms were made of linen and animal intestines. In 1870 America, vulcanized condoms could be bought from mail-order houses. *Photograph courtesy of Randy Silverman.*

gleaned from Indian women, using "mixtures of cedar sprouts, Seneca snakeroot, juniper, or [the magical plant] mug wort."[18] Black root and cedar root were also used as abortifacient agents, as well as purgatives, feminine herbal mixtures and any number of sharp instruments and rods.

According to the online source *Notes from the Frontier*, "Tablets of tinctures of pennyroyal, rue, foxglove, angelica root or partridge berry," known as squaw vine, an evergreen herb found at the base of trees and stumps, were used as abortifacients or preventives.[19]

Beginning in the 1850s, women's magazines flooded the market with feminine contraceptive products. But when the controversial 1873 Comstock Law (for the Suppression of Vice) was enacted, it restricted individuals from selling, distributing or including information about things considered obscene (such as material about contraception and abortions) through the mail.[20] And until 1969, this law limited women's reproductive rights and freedom.

Condoms for men, made from linen or animal and fish intestines and imported from Europe, were expensive. In 1830, the American self-taught chemist and engineer Charles Goodyear developed vulcanization technology, making natural rubber more durable. Within nine years, he began manufacturing "condoms, intrauterine [contraceptive] devices, douching syringes, womb veils [used in women for birth control]" and male caps and later added "gonorrhea bags," according to author Andrea Tone in *Devices and Desires: A History of Contraceptives in America*.[21]

Since this grew into a mail-order business for Goodyear, who could afford the contraceptive contrivances, with a slow stagecoach delivery (before the horse and rider of the 1860 Pony Express), how many contraceptives made their way to the western frontier, and how many male customers seeking sex used these precautions? Moreover, for the working girl who depended on turning a profit with each customer she served, how realistic were these devices that cut into her time and earnings? Since money was (and is) the thrust of the sex trade, sinking revenues from lost time, coupled with impatient and indignant customers who ran afoul of madams and saloon owners who extracted their expenses from the prostitute, if a sex worker didn't fulfill her quota, she could easily be shown the door.

According to historian Jan MacKell's *Red Light Women of the Rocky Mountains*, "In 1874, it was estimated that one out of every 18.5 persons in the United Stated had syphilis," and nearly "half of all mining camp prostitutes had suffered from the illness."[22]

In the sometimes hostile, wild and extensive reaches of the new frontier, these numbers could have been higher. What statistics can be ciphered for those infected while working in brothels, saloons, bars, dancehalls, tents, wagons or wherever else on their own? Finding themselves out of work, perhaps losing their lodgings, downgraded to working dirt streets, left alone and infected, how many women became destitute, destined to spend years in possible misery, pain and disfigurement, only to become part of an invisible and forgotten population?

Poisonous Cures

Guaiacum: as early as the sixteenth century, Girolamo Fracastoro's syphilis poem described the use of guaiacum to treat syphilis. When the resin from the hard, oily wood of the tropical evergreen tree is ingested, its sudorific properties promote sweating and help rebalance a patient's humours.

In his comprehensive article on early treatments for syphilis, appearing in the *Journal of Military and Veterans Health*, writer John Frith underscored Fracastoro's treatment and how and when to drink a guaiacum potion.[23]

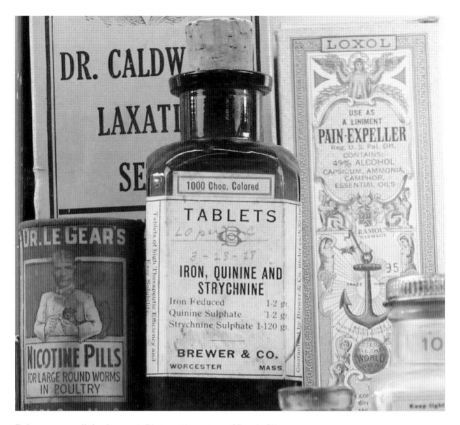

Poisonous medicinal cures? *Photograph courtesy of Randy Silverman.*

Taken twice a day, "in the morning at sunrise and by the light of the evening star," in a room shielded from wind and cold, the effectiveness of treatment lasts "until the moon completes its orbit and after the space of a month conjoins again with the sun."

Mercury

Guaiacum was discredited as a cure by Swiss physician and alchemist Paracelsus (born Theophrastus von Hohenheim in 1493), who promoted the medicinal use of mercury to treat syphilis.

John Frith explained Paracelsus's insight into mercury's poisonous properties if ingested as a potion, which prompted him to make "an ointment from metallic mercury to rub into the skin or for suffumigation [burning a substance to create vapors] for the infected to inhale or be bathed in fumes or indeed both at the same time."

During a mercury treatment, a patient is placed in a heated room, rubbed and massaged several times a day with mercury ointment poultices and left beside a sweltering fire to sweat out the body's impurities. This process was repeated for weeks, months or even years.

Mercury's efficacy—the sore mouth ulcers, the extent of patients dying of mercurial poisoning rather than from syphilis and the progression of other toxic elements used in the mix, like arsenic and vitriol—came into question. All gave credibility to the adage: "A night with Venus, a lifetime with Mercury."

Syphilis was a frightening and dangerous disease that triggered the invention of precarious, myth-loaded cures. Some infected men might have suffocated in the steam baths before they could be restored to health. Others tried to safeguard their children and wives by surreptitiously mixing mercury-laced chocolate sodas to drink, but that was reckless. And the fabled act of having sex with virgins to rid oneself of the dreadful disease only broadened its transmission.

For nearly 450 years and into the nineteenth century, mercury played a prominent role in the medical practice of treating syphilis. Different variations of the odorless, white, powdered, mercurous chloride-based calomel, once called "the miracle drug" (later termed "worm candy," as it was used to treat parasites) was touted to treat various disorders, from bronchitis and tuberculosis to gout, ingrown toenails, cancer and syphilis. It, too, produced undesirable reactions, including excessive amounts of salivation, the breakdown of cheek and gum tissues, tooth loss and severe diarrhea. In high demand and in high doses, this purgative led to mercury poisoning.

Be Prepared and Overdoses

Assembling medical supplies for the Corps of Discovery's 1803–6 Lewis and Clark Expedition, a two-and-a-half-year, eight-thousand-mile trek across North America, Meriwether Lewis packed dozens of fundamental drugs. Living on diets of dried beaver tail, elk and buffalo meat, most members of the party suffered serious bouts of constipation and, having sexual wiles, were plagued by syphilis. Captain Lewis included copious amounts of the potent cathartic calomel and mercury that was used to treat syphilis.

Laudanum (made with opium, alcohol, spices and perhaps honey for taste) was taken for pain, coughs and headaches. Dr. Benjamin Rush's anti-bilious pills, containing calomel and the powdered laxative jalap, were so strong and fast-acting for constipation that they were called "Rush's thunderbolts." It's a wonder these men didn't die of dehydration.

In the 1800s, another widely taken pill or liquid that contained mercuric chloride was "blue mass." The famous blue pills were used for a variety of maladies, including syphilis. They were easily abused by people, who, self-medicating for melancholia, ratcheted up dangerous amounts of mercury in their systems.

Treatments containing chemical elements like tellurium, platinum and gold were quickly offered and were just as swiftly considered ineffective. For better or for worse, since people were married to the potentially curing powers of the infamous "quick silver," mercury remained at the forefront of fighting syphilis.

Since these treatments were expensive, how would a frontier prostitute even know about such cures, let alone be able pay for these drugs that could potentially kill them?

RACING FOR THE SAFE CURE

In 1905, German zoologist Fritz Richards Schaudinn and dermatologist Erick Hoffman discovered the syphilis-causing bacterium now known as *Treponema pallidum*. The following year, German bacteriologist Paul von Wassermann developed a blood test, the "Wassermann reaction," to detect syphilis.[24]

Four years later, after 605 unsuccessful trials, working with arsenic compounds as a replacement for mercury to treat syphilis, German histological chemist Paul Ehrlich and his assistant, Japanese bacteriologist Sahachiro Hata, found success in chemical no. 606, an arsenic preparation (arsphenamine). Called Salvarsan, if used in the early phases of syphilis, it killed specific microbes (bacteria) without harming the patient. Although Salvarsan injections were painful and required more injections throughout the year, by 1910, the "magic bullet" was in the marketplace.[25]

In 1928, penicillin was discovered in a London lab by Scottish scientist Alexander Fleming.[26] Since he did not have the funds to develop it into a working drug, other scientists strove to purify penicillin for over a decade without success.

The turning point in the treatment of syphilis (and gonorrhea) appeared in 1943 at the U.S. Marine Hospital, when, Frith explained, "penicillin, a group of bacteria-fighting antibiotics, was successfully used to treat patients in the first or second stage, exhibiting 'primary syphilis chancres with intermuscular injections of penicillin every four hours for eight days,'" by which time, syphilitic sufferers were cured.

Prostitutes endured. As thousands of workers flooded the young western Utah region, the business of prostitution expanded into Utah's cities and towns, forts, settlements, boroughs and burgs and mountain mining camps near railways, depots and junctions—wherever there were men, wherever there were needs.

3

KATE FLINT

Folk Hero and Sinner

*T*t is a shadowy business, the one that involves a brothel-running madam selling sex in a territory that later became a state and flummoxed community that not only called her evil but acquiesced to her presence. In repugnance, the community levied fines that shored up the city's economy and doled out, for luckless prostitutes, the aberration of abatement. This occurred when Salt Lake City police judge and alderman Jeter Clinton sentenced Kate Flint for operating a house of ill-fame on Commercial Steet, a ruling which she did not take lying down.

The Burg on the Bear

Rumored to have serviced troops near the 2,500-acre Fort Douglas that was built in 1862 on the east bank overlooking Salt Lake City, Ms. Flint wound her way to the new and predominantly non-Mormon town of Corinne in Box Elder County.

Some sixty miles northwest of Salt Lake City, Corinne was founded in 1869 by the Union Pacific Railroad, former Union army officers, entrepreneurs and citizen "gentiles" who were reeling from LDS president Brigham Young's 1866 devastating prohibition of trade with non-Mormon merchants and bankers.[27]

Corinne was a wild western town with a political future. *Photograph used with permission from the Utah State Historical Society.*

The town's founders aspired to expand trade into Wyoming, Idaho and Montana; export Utah goods; create a viable city; and, according to historian Brigham D. Madsen, "break the economic and political monopoly held by the Mormons in the Utah Territory."[28] They believed Corinne could become the new state capital of Utah.

Corinne's epoch was about location and opportunity. In 1869, the transcontinental railroad was completed, with a depot elevating Corinne's status. The town became a transfer point for the railway and the terminus and subsequent trade route for wagoners transporting goods on the Montana–Idaho trail. An active north–south railroad junction, ore from as far as Bannock, Montana, could be hauled to Corinne, loaded onto the railroad cars and freighted to San Francisco for overseas shipment to Swansea, Wales.

Since the town was located on the west bank of the Bear River, leading to the north shore of the Great Salt Lake, its proximity also guaranteed an enviable setting as a veritable maritime port in the desert. A modern, three-hundred-ton, $40,000 steamboat called the *City of Corinne* was soon heralded to sail "the briny deep," initiating vigorous commercial water travels.

TROUBLED WATERS

This country's remarkable transportation feat aside, President Brigham Young was troubled. He denounced the proliferation of railroad towns and the countless travelers, laborers, miners, railroad workers, shippers, freighters, carpetbaggers and speculators, which foretold escalating numbers of "gentiles" descending on the Mormons. Bandied about were descriptions of foreseeable chaos: "unblushing depravity," gambling halls, saloons and debauchery. He wanted to "freeze them out," and he was not alone.

In *Corinne: The Gentile Capital of Utah*, historian Brigham H. Madsen quotes Brigham Young, predicting "the destruction of Zion unless some kinds of control were exercised over the gentile storekeepers who were beginning to crowd into Utah."[29]

Union Pacific owned myriad lots as compensation for surveying and platting the one-mile-square site. General Williamson, the elected town mayor, auctioned off these and other parcels and, within a week, sold over

$100,000 worth of property. From spare grasslands, Corinne grew into an urban society incorporated as a "third-class city," consisting of more than five hundred framed structures, tents, business enterprises and a steadily growing population of 1,500 inhabitants. A free public school was established there, and a proliferation of churches of different faiths—Episcopalian, Methodist, et cetera—offered services. Polygamy was outlawed within the city limits, and a strict law banned the carrying of concealed weapons and the shooting of firearms in the street.

That said, in its youth, Corinne was indeed a raw western town of "blood and thunder" repute, grappling with lawlessness and disorder. Some people called it the "Little Chicago of the West." Rife with alcohol and "vinous spirituous liquors" flowing from its twenty-eight saloons, Corinne was ripe with licentious and beckoned nymphs du pave, soiled doves, crib workers

An 1867 view of the great Salt Lake City. *Photograph used with permission from the Utah State Historical Society.*

and brothels and dance house owners, likely introducing burlesque acts with "ruffled underpants," bare legs and can-can flexibility. The town also apparently attracted one gun-toting town marshal.

Corinne provided entertainment and distraction for constant streams of floating populations—those very miners, railroad men, gandy dancers, shippers, freighters—along with a dedicated sporting crowd that came from as far away as Elko. If one craved culture, this town obliged. In 1870, a steady flow of stock companies traveling on the transcontinental railroad to California would stop at Corinne's newly built opera house, where they performed tableaux vivants (posed and stilled living pictures), séances, musical renditions and plays like *Hamlet* and *The Lady of Lyons* to packed audiences in the dimly lit theater. No firearms were allowed.

Mormons called Corinne the "City of the Un-Godly." It was a bustling municipality of short-lived infamy.[30] For Kate Flint, it was a mighty appealing calling card. Seizing on the opportunity to sell sex, she opened a brothel, acquired three inmates, settled in and profitably served a constant source of traffic until she changed course and headed to Salt Lake City's large and rebellious red-light district.

In-and-Out-of-Sight

Ms. Flint ran brothels on Salt Lake City's Commercial Street (later known as Regent Street), a fifty-foot-wide block-long area that cut between Main Street and State Street. It was bordered by 100 South and 200 South Streets and was a lively set-up infused with brothels, parlors, independent prostitutes, streetwalkers and hens (house inmates).[31] A fractious component of the city's tenderloin (underworld) district, legitimate businesses straddled the ground floor; prostitutes and madams lived in or worked on the second floor. The buffered, somewhat tucked-in enclave was a bustling hotbed for customers from all walks of life and religion. Their lustful activities were mostly hidden and unobserved by regular pedestrians walking outside the block on Main Street.

Considered pretty and young, Kate Flint might have been around twenty-five years old when she arrived in Salt Lake City. She was born in Ireland (or Tennessee, where her parents lived). Her age and name may have been cheeky lies. But her independence and business know-how were striking and never more so than when she was faced with a series of fines, threats and the sudden abatement (or smashup) of her home.

Commercial Street (now Regent Street), 1903. *Photograph used with permission from the Utah State Historical Society.*

An Arresting Case

During a routine raid on August 28, 1872, the city's police arrested Kate Flint (and neighboring keeper Cora Conway) for running brothels. Facing Justice Jeter Clinton, both women were found guilty. Ms. Flint was fined fifteen dollars (Cora was fined less). When Clinton realized that many previous fines had not discouraged Flint—nor any other prostitute, for that matter—from leaving town, he levied the penalty to one hundred dollars.

In a recap of those August events, the March 13, 1875 *Salt Lake Herald-Republican* wrote, "Justice Clinton…told [Kate] that so long [as] she paid the fines, she might 'run' her house, but when she refused to pay, his boys 'would do her great injury.'"

Several days earlier, Ms. Flint had paid a one-hundred-dollar fine. She offered fifty dollars and, after thinking it over, questioned the number of charges she had taken care of. She asked for a receipt, about which the paper reported, "He said if he gave her one, he would be put out of office." Kate would not budge.

"Clinton kept her there for some time, telling her that he could not make out the appeal bond [until] the city attorney returned." The *Herald-Republican* continued, "Finally, the justice told her she could go home, and nothing would be done [until] the morning." But Clinton had already done something. Deeming her home a nuisance, he ordered it abated. When Flint returned to her house, she found the smashup was near completion.

During the court-ordered abatement of Flint's home, Salt Lake City was thick and vocal in "the struggle going on in Utah between the opposing elements of vice and virtue—the latter represented by the local civic authorities backed by the united sentiment of the majority of the people and the former by saloon men, gamblers and prostitutes, encouraged in their lawlessness by the anti-Mormon ring and all but openly challenged by officials of the federal government," wrote Mormon historian and LDS apostle Orson F. Whitney in the *History of Utah*.[32]

The Dastardly Done Deed

An imposing individual at over six feet tall, Brigham Young Hampton was tasked, alongside the "church-dominated police force" and a posse of nine men, with carrying out the abatement of Flint's home.

Mr. Hampton, a religious and "modestly successful businessman," was a committed chronicler of his experiences, observations, successes, failures, beliefs and family life. Retrieved from various archival sources and called "narratives," Hampton's personal writings were illuminated in *Kingdom in the West*, "Voices of Dissent," in which editors Polly Aird, Jeff Nichols and Will Bagley emphasized the man's unequivocal allegiance to Latter-day Saint convictions.[33] "He played a starring role in many public dramas during the Mormon-gentile conflict that raged from the Utah War of 1857 until the state's admission to the Union in 1896," the editors wrote. Eager to live in his faith and prepared to fight to defend his church, Hampton's narrative was drenched in the prevalent religious community's commonly held distrust and intense abhorrence of those not of their faith.

"For the next three-plus decades, Mormons struggled with merchants, miners, attorneys and journalists to control the territory," the editors explained. "The bitterness of this conflict vividly stamps the pages of Hampton's story…that is full of aspersions on 'sinister' gentiles."

Venerated as a saint among Mormons, Hampton was considered by many non-Mormons a "latter-day thug."

A House Upheaval

Amid the household items that were broken, axed, kicked in, tossed, taken, soiled or stolen, Flint stepped into the turbulence of a house asunder. If one small table managed to survive, at least tenfold of the previously existing furniture, fixtures, white goods, fabrics, lamps—nearly everything in her private home and brothel—was wrecked and dumped into haphazard, most likely illegal, colossal piles of rubbish.

Mr. Hampton was clearing out the contents of Kate's bureau when she walked into her room. Presumably, he told her to claim her articles of clothing. Some of the house prostitutes had done just that, collecting their belongings and even hers. But she didn't—and why would she? If it were not a matter of who had handled her clothing and personal items, what could she say or rescue that might later be held against her? Asking about a wad of money she had cached in her bureau was pointless; she could see it wasn't there. Finding her bank book, though, was a stroke of good luck. Flint left with it. But her home was now uninhabitable, and the means of support for its inmates were scorched. As for the leftovers? There were some unriffled items left stored in the basement that Ms. Flint soon sought to sell for pennies on the dollar. And then she waited.

A Reign of Polarization: A Field Day for Newspapers

On August 30, 1872, the *Corinne Journal Reporter*'s headline howled, "Wanton Destruction of Property," as it sharply defied Jeter Clinton, the "Mormon police justice," who

> ordered the destruction of [two] houses of ill-fame keepers [Kate] *Flint*
> *and* [Cora] *Conway, and immediately thereafter,* [a] *posse of Danites*
> [a vigilante group of Avenging Angels] *proceeded to carry out the*

edict of the ruffian who exercises judicial functions in the city of sin. The
property of [the] woman was taken out and demolished piecemeal by the
police, and soon, total wreck replaced what was before the home of the
unfortunate occupants.

In a harangue, the same paper disparaged Brigham Young, "The chief manager of prostitution stood looking on, grandly exempt from the havoc touching the many stinking bagnios [brothels] over which he is ruler. The sins of Commercial Street, where the property was destroyed, are classed as nuisances, while the houses of ill-fame, supported by the Prophet and his lecherous 'priests,' are safe, for the present."

The *Deseret Evening News* rebuffed such a reaction on August 30, 1872, stressing a common fear among the populace: "For it has been easily seen that those who plied these [evil] vocations were becoming more brazen and defiant and were creating a public opinion to sustain and justify them in their vile traffic. Let such practices flourish, and how long would it take to produce a demoralization of sentiment here that their continued existence would be demanded as a necessary evil?"

The paper expressed gratitude for the police officers who performed "the [abatement] duty imposed upon them by law…done at time when it was so much needed that the feeling among the great majority of our citizens is one of satisfaction and relief."

The paper also reinforced the prevalent belief among its many citizens:

The undivided sentiment here, up to the past few years, was a favor of
the marriage of the sexes, in utter opposition to harlotry. That sentiment
is still entertained by a very large majority of the people of Utah. They
still desire their sons to be husbands, not paramours; their daughters to be
wives, not harlots.

After Ms. Flint was arrested, the August 29, 1872 *Salt Lake Tribune* stated, "The Social Evil and Arrest of the Demi-Monde [recognized] prostitution as a social evil as the race itself, deplored as well by the outside world." But it said that all philosophical, social and governmental attempts to solve the problem have "failed to blot it out—as evidenced by the experience of the centuries."

The paper then questioned why. "[A]re the means employed by our city authorities adapted to the suppression of the evil complained of? Does making prostitution a source of revenue tend to its overflow? To accept from the fallen woman her ill-gotten gains look more like pandering to prostitution for the sake of its spoils than a disposition to suppress it."

Under the headline "The City Authorities and the Demi-Monde" that appeared the following day, the *Salt Lake Tribune*, which "did not justify or uphold houses of ill-fame," laid bare its thinking on illegal abatement, religious fanaticism and extortion. The article maintained the "wanton and malicious destruction of the frail ones of Commercial Street" was a riotous proceeding that violated the laws of the United States, "not prompted out of the desire for producing a 'better state of morals in the city' but simply out of revenge at not being able to control the entire earnings of the women from their life of shame."

The article stressed the presupposed extremism among what was considered by the liberal paper and others as both a polygamic city council and a polygamic police court. "So long as Jeter and a few of the police could pocket handsome prerequisites and be sharers in the money—providing there was enough or it—sentimentally and morality were left out of the question, and houses of ill fame were unmolested."

Tackling the fraught issue of vice and virtue shadowed by religious creed, the *Salt Lake Tribune* remained stalwart: "The lascivious evils of Commercial Street have never equaled the lasciviousness of marrying mother and daughter, two sisters, or many other of the abominations of polygamic intercourse, yet this species of licentiousness is called religion, and its advocates are those who are attempting to legislate and enforce virtue on those whose passions are not satiated by a divine license."

An Outraged Justice Speaks

Jeter Clinton wasn't certain the act of demolishing a home of ill-repute was strong or harsh enough. Quoting passages from "Sermon Delivered by Dr. Jeter Clinton," which was reprinted in the reputed-to-be-anti-Mormon *Expositor*, he may have set out to defend his "controversial abatement" charge.[34]

> *The Jews and gentiles have driven us from place to place, and they have tried to drive us out, but I can tell you, friends, that we are not going from here.....Now for these women, the low, nasty street-walkers...the low, nasty, dirty, filthy, stinking bitches...that will invite strange men into their houses and introduce them into their family circles...their excuse was that they were boarders, but that is a lie....They ought to be shot with a double-*

barrel shot-gun....That is my doctrine....And when you see these ~~street walkers~~ [men] *following behind such women (God keep me from calling them women), take a double-barreled shot-gun and follow them, shoot them to pieces; and if you do not overtake them before they get to their haunts or dens, kill them both.*

SILENCE

While newspapers and periodicals railed, Ms. Flint, who kept her personal life and business dealings close to her chest, remained some distance from the press. According to historian Jeffrey Nichols, "The abatement of her home did not drive the women [Ms. Flint and Cora Conway] from the city."[35] Ms. Conway, pale and suffering from the raid, reportedly retired as a brothel keeper and worked as a prostitute in other houses, including Ms. Flint's. Within four months, though, Ms. Flint was back to business and silently waiting for her time in front of third district court judge James B. McKean, who was "an avowed enemy of polygamy."

MARCH 1875: A CLASH OF IDEALS

It was mostly lion and little lamb that March, and there was less reconciliation between the two classes of Mormon and gentile citizens. Even though numbers of each group held similar thoughts about the sale of sex, they didn't publicly bring about open communal discussions. Instead, the city roiled with rancor, suspicion and righteous spite in an environment consistently influenced by the authoritative social structure of the LDS Church. In Utah's efforts to join the union, defending polygamy loomed as a federal and personal quagmire for Mormons. At the same time, free speech and vital dissention surfaced as a value at great risk among gentiles.

The Mormons contended "divinely sanctioned plural marriage" was a blessed virtue, far from the depravity of prostitution. Liberal papers punted back that polygamy involved multiple women and prostitution, multiple men, "and both constituted a crime of 'plural cohabitation.'"[36]

In an environment in which one can't trust another who is not of their ilk, letters of aversion become common, such as the opinion in the March 13, 1875 *Salt Lake Tribune*'s "City Jottings": "A sister said yesterday she was going to petition [Mormon convert] Bishop Axtoll for the removal of Judge

McKean and after removing him, have him indicted and hung up by the probate court. This infliction," the paper added, "was upon the chief justice, because he sent Bro. Brigham to the penitentiary."

Yes, Judge McKean did that temporarily; it had something to do with an alimony case brought before him by Ann Eliza Web Young, Brigham Young's nineteenth wife. Charging her husband with "neglect, cruelty and desertion," Ann asked for a certain amount of alimony that provoked Young to call her nothing but an extortionist and insisted that they were never married—nor would they be in the eyes of the law. It was a cliffhanger, all right.[37]

Later that month, the *Salt Lake Tribune* was "threatened." And on March 20, 1875, the paper thundered a response to the attack:

> *Last Sunday, the ward orators broke out in a fresh place. This pestiferous gentile sheet still troubled their souls, and in order that serenity might be restored to their minds and quiet to the kingdom, they all, with one accord, pronounced* THE TRIBUNE *a nuisance and declared that it must be abated.*

"It can be easily understood," the *Salt Lake Tribune* roared on, "that a free newspaper published in such a community must be regarded as obnoxious and revolutionary. It is the clash of two deadly opposites. Light and darkness….But we know this is all froth and foul air. THE *TRIBUNE* office will not be sacked. Freedom of speech cannot be destroyed with the wreck of a few cases of metal and the breaking up of a printing press…and we will never cease in our agitation and antagonism until they are fully accorded."

Flint Speaks Her Mind

In the meantime, the threatened Judge James B. McKean retired from the bench but not before hearing Kate Flint's case against Jeter Clinton, et al., in a suit for "alleged malicious destruction of plaintiff's property" on March 14, 1875.[38]

When the first jury selection was made, Flint and her lawyer Robert Baskin objected, believing they could not have a fair trial with all Mormon jurists—most certainly when all the defendants were Mormon. "[Ms. Flint] claimed the LDS Church specifically targeted her because she was 'known as one who is opposed to the same and has incurred its displeasure and hostility,'" wrote Nichols.[39]

After a balanced jury comprised of Mormons and gentiles was finally selected and approved, a list of lengthy propositions was prepared by the defendants for the court to instruct the jury. Most specifically, the March 15, 1875 *Deseret Evening News* reported that the first assertion stated, "By common law, territorial statute and a valid ordinance of Salt Lake City, bawdy houses were made common nuisances and could be abated by law." The last assertion addressed the court to "instruct the jury that before the plaintiff could obtain these damages claimed, an indictment must be found and conviction secured against the defendants in the suit for the alleged criminal act. The court refused to so instruct."

The plaintiff's counsel propositions were brief, addressing the destruction of property, liability and an illegal warrant ordering the destruction without authority of law.[40]

Ms. Flint was prepared for this trial. She listed every piece of personal property that had been wantonly destroyed by the callousness of the police, along with her significant loss of cash and the devastation that occurred when she walked into her home, shocked by the abatement that she was assured would not be taking place at the time. Witness after witness was called. Brigham Young Hampton testified. More people were sworn in. Rebuttals ramped up. By noon, much was laid to rest.

While the March 15 and 16, 1875 *Salt Lake Tribune* reported the jury struggled twice, unable to agree on a verdict, the March 15 *Deseret Evening News* conveyed the judge's statement that destroying property in such a manner, as had been done, "was not proper," making clear his position:

> *If Kate Flint kept a house and it was proved that fifty men frequented for purposes of illicit intercourse, and the process could be issued, and her furniture and household goods be broken up therefor[e], the same could be done with John Smith, who might have in his house twelve women with whom he had illicit sexual intercourse. It would not matter whether he claimed that those women were his wives, the law allowed a man but one wife, and, had a justice of the peace the right to act as in the case of Kate Flint, it would not alter the situation if Kate Flint claimed that the fifty or more men visiting her house were her husbands. Such a case would not take it outside of the law; and neither would be in the case of the polygamist. Whatever might be thought of polygamy, the sending of officers into the houses of those practicing it to demolish furniture and effects was not the proper way to deal with it. In dealing with that or any other questions, the limits of the law must be respected.*

Commenting on the destruction of Ms. Flint's home, the court ruled that the warrant was indeed illegal, and judgment was eventually delivered: $6,000 settled both Ms. Flint's claim with $3,400 and Ms. Conway's with $2,600. The Mormon community was apoplectic with rage. Kate Flint reopened her house.

She Had a Husband?

A well-connected and "mannerly man" welcomed by many, the congenial D. Frank Connelly traveled extensively throughout the West. In 1880, he purchased and deeded to Flint a parcel near East 200 South Street on Victoria Place, where she opened what may have been the area's first brothel. Mr. Connelly later selected two adjacent lots from David Frederick Walker of the Walker Brothers Bank and conveyed them to Flint.

According to Nichols, D. Frank Connelly was a player, venturer and consummate gambler who was devoted to horses, horse racing, alcohol, good food and Kate. Still, it was startling to learn that the enigmatic woman had been secretly married to this sporting man who helped her business and real estate prosper until he died in 1884 at the age of forty-six, unknown to others, in Kate's brothel.[41]

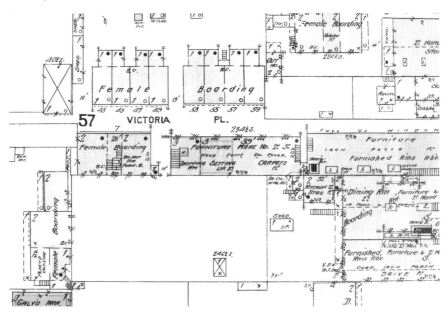

Victoria Place in the red-light district. *The Sanborn maps.*

Mr. Connelly was buried in Salt Lake City's Mount Olivet Cemetery. Baptist minister Dr. Dewitt conducted the service, and the treasured man's elaborately designed casket was carried by eight pallbearers. A munificent display of flowers, "wrought into all shapes imaginable [were] laid on the casket and floral wreaths, anchors and hearts were deposited on the grave."[42] Mr. Connelly's tall and stately stone sepulcher is softened by an intriguing, winged angel that is carrying chains to her beloved's side.

After the funeral, Kate wrote a public note of thanks: "Will you permit me through your columns to express my thanks to those who assisted in the funeral services and those who, by their presence and otherwise, contributed toward the respectful demonstration on the occasion of my late husband's obsequies. To all sincere thanks, Mrs. D. Connelly."

Recognized as one of the most beautiful cemeteries in the West, Mount Olivet Cemetery was designated "as a burial place for all people" by an act of Congress in 1874, signed by President Ulysses S. Grant. A public nonprofit cemetery, it nearly tripled in size, and its eighty-eight acres are home to historic clusters of old, broad trees, parcels of curious deer and groups of wild rabbits, with small gnawers and lofty hawks creating a sense of harmony and life among the many tombstones, graves, mausoleums, vaults, burial chambers and monuments tied to this earth.

There are many angels in cemeteries, even some with chains and open wings. Various lore tenders have many interpretations. Angels are spiritual messengers between God and man. They guard the soul. Weeping angels grieve for the departed and those who suffered untimely deaths. Angels with horns herald judgment day. Angels with open wings accompany souls to heaven. Chains and anchors reflect safety, symbolizing hope; they also represent seamanship. Broken chains designate the end of life.

Connelly's angel, 138 years later, is weatherworn, her facial features whittled down by Utah winds and cold. But her posture and bare shoulders; the concrete folds of her dress; the heavy chains she holds in her hands that flow past her wrist, encircle her waist and fit into an anchor set upon the stone; and her solid wings show strength and devotion.

Kate's chains, if designed by her, are unbroken and carefully held. Her head and stance appear resolute. The connection between the lover and the madam was unwavering. Her open wings seem capable of holding the two of them in any kind of weather. But who knows what Kate was thinking.

An angel in chains and anchor holds on D. Frank Connelly's tombstone in Mount Olivet Cemetery. *Photograph courtesy of the author.*

1885: ANOTHER OF BJH'S MORAL MISADVENTURE

An avid member of a citizens' committee chaired by Francis Armstrong, in May 1885, Mr. Hampton was asked to flesh out those involved in lewd and lascivious conduct, including those "government officials and others in the 'hoardoms' and adultery and bring them to justice if the money was furnished to do the work," Hampton wrote in his diary. "I told him I would do my best."[43]

Hiring two women, Fanny "Devenport" and S.J. Field, as detectives, Mr. Hampton set them up to conduct sexual business in brothels on West Temple Street. He rented rooms from the madams who managed these houses of ill-fame and was depicted as using chambers connected "with several other rooms and by 'apitures' in the doors and walls [to catch] the 'beastile' conduct of men and women 'gowing' to such houses for illicit intercourse."

The earnest man worked with twenty-five male volunteers and paid the fabricated detectives $300 to $400 for their services.[44] He claimed about one hundred men were caught: regular joes, a smattering of government officials, a Baptist minister he called "Dewit" and a female leader of the church's choir (who were both spiritually there to preach—right place, wrong time) and a dozen or so married Mormon men who were deemed well on their way to becoming apostates. Others were protected from exposure.

Such efforts spawned a failed coup and were brought to court—Mormon merchant and city selectman Francis Armstrong would testify to bankrolling the citizens' committee service with $500—with devastating results. The warrant was invalid. Charges were brought. The female detectives who closed shop and skedaddled to Denver were ordered back to the Salt Lake City court to testify. Mr. Hampton volunteered to take full responsibility. Indicted for conspiracy in December and for keeping houses of ill-fame, he was sentenced to one year of imprisonment in the county jail, where, the poor man wrote, he was "furnished with three meals a day at the expense of one dollar a day to the county, treated as well as anyone [person] could wish being a prisoner" and, after his time was served, was freed. Amen.

AND KATE?

In 1886, Kate Flint was again in court, pleading guilty to keeping a house of ill-fame. She paid her fine and shuttered her house; she was maybe in jail for ten days and might have said she would retire then and there.

This was apparently not the case. Running vigil over her husband's grave, Ms. Flint ran the two-story adobe building on Victoria Place that was gifted to her by him and accessible via a discreet alleyway. Two years later, she sold the building and moved to Social Hall Avenue, where she meant to comfortably retire, her future secure with extensive real estate holdings and houses rented to other keepers of ill-fame until the turn of the century.

While she was a highly regarded prostitute folk legend in the red-light district, who really knew the madam and what her next move, if taken, would be?

4

NO DEARTH OF CUSTOMERS

*I*n the late 1840s, when the new frontier west of the Missouri River opened the floodgates of opportunity and adventure—the Utah Territory in the thick of it—droves of prospectors, miners, railway men and, eventually, carpetbaggers and others raced in pursuit of the promises emanating from this wild and barely discovered (by white settlers) outland. Far from home and lonely in an environment where women were scarce, it wasn't long before prostitutes followed to ply their trade.

In the late 1850s, prostitution spread into Utah's rural settlements, military forts and camps. Called "camp followers," prostitutes, bar girls and even actresses arrived to entertain the troops. They worked near military bases and camps, such as Colonel Albert Sidney Johnston's 2,400–3,000 troops in the Utah Expedition at Camp Floyd, which was connected to the town of Fairfield during what was called the Utah War.

CAMP FLOYD

The Johnston camp was built after Brigham Young, irate about "charges [made] against his people" by the federal government, of which he had no say, declared a state of martial law in 1857.

Johnson's troops were "not [there] to fight renegade Indians but to quell a reported insurrection among a group of white Americans," wrote Thomas

C.E. Johnson, *A Good Time. Photograph courtesy of the Special Collections, Merrill-Cazier Library, Utah State University.*

G. Alexander and Leonard J. Arrington in their article "Camp in the Sagebrush: Camp Floyd Utah."[45]

Built by soldiers, Mormon laborers and skilled craftsmen, "Fairfield and Camp Floyd's population boomed quickly to become one of the largest cities in the Utah territory." Alexander and Arrington described Frogtown, adjacent to Fairfield, as having "seventeen saloons [and] an accouterment of gamblers, prostitutes, slickers [swindlers] and thieves." Fairfield's main street was reminiscent of California gold rush–era mining towns "lined with drinking and gambling saloons."

Although Camp Floyd was a "boon to Utah's economy," as Utahns sold goods and services to Johnson's Camp Floyd and bought back the goods at steeply reduced prices, Alexander and Arrington explained that some "troops and camp followers were responsible for the inauguration of the problems which has adverse [e]ffects on the Mormon community":

> *Some officers tried to induce women to* [come] *to Camp Floyd to engage in prostitution, and one officer actually sought to proposition the mistress of a household in which he was a guest. Camp followers and troops often made nuisance of themselves in Salt Lake City and other settlements, and* [an occasional] *murder resulted from the activities of these men....The church leadership was so concerned that Wilford Woodruff of the Council of Twelve Apostles exhorted the church membership to restrain themselves and not to mingle with the wicked.*

A variety of entertainments were introduced to help distract the soldiers who were living in unfamiliar western environs. The camp's social hall was built by a German singing group. A theater on base welcomed traveling actors. According to Alexander and Arrington, "A soldiers' circus company with acrobatic and equestrian acts gave a number of performances. Military personnel from Camp Floyd organized Utah's first Masonic lodge, and post officers erected a billiard hall, held dances and enjoyed horse racing."

School classes were taught. A temperance society was organized. Independent soldiers and officers took to the desert to learn about "whirlwinds, electric phenomena and cloud formations." Some men painted in oil, while others sketched camp life scenes. Bible studies were held in German and English, and opportunities to learn the Shoshonean language were offered and taken. Acres of land were planted. Soldiers honed their military skills. And spare time was absorbed in prospecting for silver, lead and gold. "Evidence shows that the first claims filed in Tooele County were not filed by Patrick Connor's California volunteers, as is usually claimed, but by members of the Utah Expedition," Alexander and Arrington explained.

According to historian Audrey M. Godfrey's *Utah History Encyclopedia* article, "Camp Floyd," the troops "improved western immigrant roads and existing trails. A detachment escorted the seventeen surviving children of the Mountain Meadows Massacre to Fort Leavenworth. Others guarded army paymasters and immigrant trains between Utah and California."[46]

Camp Floyd was renamed Fort Crittenden after it was discovered its namesake was a sympathizer with the Confederacy, and it was abandoned in 1861. But there was a rush to trade sex for money during the few years it existed, and among the sheer volume of soldiers and crowds of visiting male merchants, traders and speculators in that dust-riddled camp ensured there was no dearth of customers. Later, the same held true for some remote mining towns, like Frisco—until there was trouble.

Frisco

In the late 1870s, the once-booming mining town of Frisco, located near the Horn Silver Mine in the San Francisco Mountains in Beaver County, Utah, was considered one of the "wildest mining camps in the West," wrote Miriam B. Murphy in the January 1996 *History Blazer*.[47]

By 1875, in the town inhabited by several thousand residents, a place where drinking water had to be brought in, there were twenty-one to twenty-three saloons, "gambling dens and houses of prostitution." Murders occurred there nearly every day. The town's two morticians were indispensable. Wagons were often brought out to pick up bodies before taking them to Boot Hill for burial. The town soon earned its reputation for being "Dodge City, Tombstone, Sodom and Gomorrah all rolled into one," Murphy wrote.

N.S. Slaughter, General Merchandise in Frisco. *Photograph used with permission from the Utah State Historical Society.*

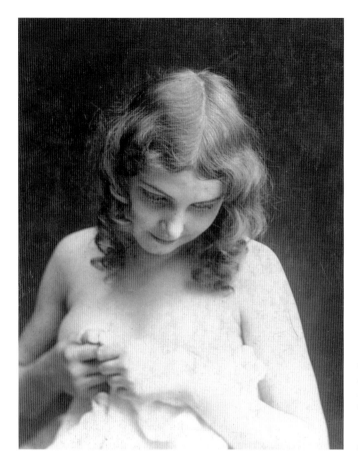

C.E. Johnson, *You See Johnson All Over the World. Photograph courtesy of the Special Collections, Merrill-Cazier Library, Utah State University.*

The town even sought "reformed quick-draw artist" Marshal John T. Pearson from Pioche, Nevada, which had its own crowded Boot Hill and flock of prostitutes and was considered the most dangerous town in the Silver State, to come in and clean up Frisco. Apparently, the man did not believe in arresting anyone, nor did he have plans to build a prison. Instead, he shot people at the first hint of a crime and supposedly "killed six outlaws on his first night in town."

Passing through the skeleton of the town in 1981, author Gode Davis wrote in "Frisco: The Story of Utah's Gomorrah," it was a "hell-raising mining town reminiscent only of San Francisco's infamous Barbary Coast District and a few places more."[48]

There were gunslingers, rowdies, drifters, gamblers, card sharks, criminals and countless working girls. "Saloons became brothels," Davis wrote. "Sexual favors doled out by perfumed tenderloin ladies, who solicited randy customers who lounged in the smoke-filled main floor, dispensed their wares in musky rooms upstairs on the second floor."

According to Davis, a variety of prostitutes took on "even the most jaded tastes," including peg-houses for homosexuals; young, imported (most likely trafficked) "Oriental slaves"; and pretty waiter girls, some of whom spoke Spanish and others who "were stolen from Indian tribes." In Frisco's "low, vicious dives, children of both sexes (as well as women) were sometimes made to perform lewd dances for the customers' pleasure."

A Thick Vein

The Horn Silver Mine was a leading producer of lead, zinc and silver in Utah. In 1880, the mine became the terminus for the Utah Southern Railroad extension from Milford that connected Frisco with the rest of the country. "During its peak years, some 150 tons of ore a day were sent to the Salt Lake Valley for smelting," Murphy wrote. "By 1885, the Horn had produced more the $13 million and paid its shareholders $4 million in dividends."

The economy was stable for most who lived in Frisco, but its character was dangerous, and it didn't help to have troubles in the mines. In February 1885, when the night shift went to work in the mines, they experienced a series of tremors. Apparently, the tunnels in the cave were not effectively timbered. As the night shift returned to the surface in the morning, they and the incoming day shift were all told to keep out of the mine. No sooner than this was said, an enormous cave-in closed the main shaft and collapsed the mine's tunnels down to the seventh level. Its impact was felt fifteen miles away in Milford. Fortunately, no one was in the mine. No one was hurt. There were no deaths, and no burials needed to be made.

However, right after the cave-in, large numbers of the Horn Silver Mine crew, reading the writing on the wall, left the mines and the town of Frisco to find work and homes elsewhere. Other men were temporarily laid off. "In a vicious cycle," Davis wrote, "smelters, charcoal kilns and pulp mills went quiet." Smelters closed. Kiln owners went bankrupt. Most stores folded. And making any kind of living was sorely challenged.

When the mines did finally get back to business, the few miners and families who were able to work and had already left Frisco commuted from Milford or moved into rough shacks that were spread out on the mine's property.

Above: The Liberty Bond Booth Bank in Frisco. *Photograph used with permission from the Utah State Historical Society.*

Opposite: Rows of idle kilns in Frisco. *Photograph used with permission from the Utah State Historical Society.*

Yes, the Horn Silver Mine slowly recovered and, in time, resumed its place as a leader in silver ore. But the wild, notorious boomtown of Frisco was fractured. Deserted and abandoned by many, including most of its buildings, stores, homes, saloons, dancehalls and brothels, along with prostitutes and their customers, it became a desert plume, a respite for snakes and a remembrance of bad whiskey; a legacy of murders and burials; an enthusiastic, gun-wielding sheriff; and a persistent calling card for a ghost town.

5

A WILDLY ROBUST BUSINESS

W hether they were called prostitutes, ladies of the night, fallen women, workers for the calling or simply soiled doves, by the 1870s, these working women tendered a robust business in (and around) the red-light district of Commercial Street in downtown Salt Lake City.

Between 100 South and 200 South Street from Main to State Streets, parlor houses and cribs stretched out among legitimate businesses, tobacco shops, liquor stores, saloons and cafés. Second-story rooms over these enterprises were rented out nightly to prostitutes, who would invite potential clients to "come up and visit," often while sitting on the stairways.

In the many refined parlor houses run by madams, there were no such displays of public solicitation. One rang an electric bell for admission and was usually greeted by a well-tailored attendant, escorted into an elegant room dressed in plush red fabrics, draperies, gilded mirrors and, often, a decked-out piano-playing man called "professor" improvising tunes reflecting (and possibly monitoring) the room's ambiance.[49]

In some parlors, the women were dressed appealingly. Beer was served in a small shot glass for a dollar.

A YOUNG OBSERVER

Born in Salt Lake City in 1889, John Held Jr. was sixteen years old when he first worked as a sports and political cartoonist for the *Salt Lake Tribune*. He

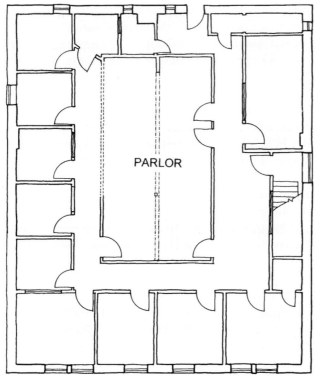

PARLOR

Above: Regent Street (formerly Commercial Street), 1938. Parlors were located on the second floor. *Photograph used with permission from the Utah State Historical Society.*

Left: Regent Street brothel. *Photograph courtesy of Thomas Carter.*

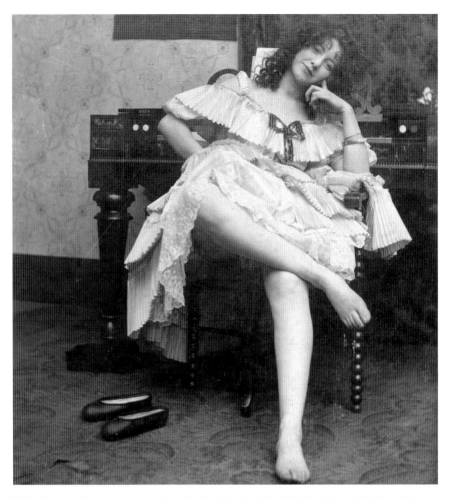

Trilby Danseuse. Photograph courtesy of the Special Collections, Merrill-Cazier Library, Utah State University.

later moved to the East Coast, where he gained national recognition for his illustrations and block prints depicting America's Jazz Age of the 1920s, à la F. Scott Fitzgerald and the "flapper" period, when free-spirited, mostly young and thin short-skirted, short-haired women rolled up their stockings, smoked from long cigarette holders and were almost always accompanied by a plumpish man with patent-leather-looking slicked-back hair, wearing a long racoon coat, carrying a hip flask and smoking a cigar.

But when Held was a kid, accompanying his uncle on calls to repair parlors' gambling machines, he had a chance to glimpse this nocturnal civilization.[50]

Brothel on the second floor of the Karrick building in Salt Lake City. The building was designed by Richard A. Kletting and built in 1887. *Photograph courtesy of the author.*

"It was said that the elegance of these palaces surpassed the lavishness of even New Orleans," wrote Held in published memoirs. "This was probably hearsay, as a gold or silver miner's or a cattle or sheep man's idea of elegance was moot in the extreme."

Ada Wilson, one of the city's earliest madams, operated a luxurious parlor house with a "professor" and his piano in its drawing room. She also took daily rides in a splendid, hackney-drawn dogcart. Helen Blazes, a more conservative madam, accommodated the wealthy and served only wine at her establishment.

Clients paid dearly for Catherine Flint's prostitutes, food and entertainment. Doggedly working her way into society, the courtesan paid close attention when items of Brigham Young's property were seized during the divorce settlement between the LDS leader and his plural wife Ann Eliza. In the November 2, 1876 issue of the *Salt Lake Tribune*, the "City Jottings" column reported, "It was rumored yesterday that Mrs. Catherine Flint had purchased Brigham's close[d] carriage and would have his coat of arms erased and her own substituted."

Prostitution was (and is) a big business. Many madams carried engraved calling cards printed by the Held Engraving Company. John Held Jr., affectionately called the "Mormon Kid," reported the demands madams made of his family's print shop: "The finest and most expensive engraving," he wrote, was printed on the best vellum stock. These cards were smaller than the social standard. They were difficult to produce by hand from a copper plate. But the run was long, "the money was fresh and there was no quibbling about price."

Expanding Boundaries

Although prostitution was deemed illegal, it was tolerated and rife in the business borough's shady backside. By the 1880s, working women had expanded Salt Lake City's boundaries from the boisterous, cosmopolitan Commercial Street and the adjacent and dimly lit Plum Alley to the racially segregated Franklin Avenue and the tenderloin district of Victoria Place.

Within a society choreographed by a subculture of prostitutes, madams, businessmen, bodyguards, politicians and unscrupulous associates, there were plenty of customers. Eager to support the sale of sex for personal satisfaction, crowds of miners, ranchers, out-of-towners, gentlemen in top hats and everyday Joes haunted the red-light district.

Plum Alley, 1907. *Photograph used with permission from the Utah State Historical Society.*

By 1886, Salt Lake City was a lively boomtown. An estimated six brothels, a series of one-night cribs, streetwalker dens, numerous saloons, dancehalls and gambling houses inundated the area and so infuriated the townspeople that they rose in protest. The police conducted raids. Clients fled. Prostitutes were arrested, checked for infections and fined. It wasn't enough, and rarely were clients' names exposed to the press.

"Occasionally, a female figure flits in from one of the side streets and is swallowed up in the darkness of Plum Alley," wrote a reporter in the October 15, 1900 issue of the *Salt Lake Tribune*. "And it needs not more than one guess from the uninitiated to tell where she has gone to." By the turn of the century, the red-light district was in full bloom. "The orchard of Salt Lake's nightlife was bearing rich, golden fruit, and it was easy pickings," John Held Jr. wrote in his memoirs. "Both Sodom and Gomorrah were paying high dividends."

When the townspeople rose in protest, the city's police conducted more raids and arrests, but there seemed no penalty strong enough to stop the tide of prostitution.

The Karrick building on Main Street in Salt Lake City. *Photograph courtesy of the author.*

Other than savvy brothel keepers, who maintained clean houses and healthy prostitutes, invested in real estate, knew the political side of doing business and had devoted partners, most working girls struggled to make ends meet. "To make any kind of a decent living, I have to take in more than one hundred dollars a month," reported a street prostitute in the December 19, 1902 issue of the *Salt Lake Herald*. "I can buy food and coal with it, pay my sixty-dollar room rent, pay the ten dollars a month required as a license [that] the police call a fine, dress myself and have spending money for cigarettes and beer."

By 1908, historian Hal Schindler wrote, "There came a hue and cry to 'clean up the city,'" and the idea of the stockade came into existence—out of sight, out of mind but still in business.

6

ASCENDING FROM BETRAYAL

PART ONE: LOVESICK

This is the story of Mary Alice Ann Devitt, who, as a pretty, blue-eyed blonde, was a free-spirited woman who seemingly knew her own mind. Waiting for the perfect man to come along, she refused to compromise. Then the charming Charlie Christianson caught her eye.

Charlie was often out of town on this or that business (maybe working for the railroad or selling door to door). No one could say exactly what the otherwise amiable man did for a living. But it was certain that Mary Alice was lovesick. Eventually, when Charlie returned from a business trip and Mary put aside her family's deeply rooted relationship with the Catholic Church, the couple was married elsewhere. Only later did Mary discover that her beloved was a bigamist. Devastated, ashamed and pregnant, Mary knew her twenty-five-year-old life was about to change. In 1884, Mary Alice disappeared.

Potato Famine and the American Dream

The youngest girl among ten siblings, Mary Alice Ann Devitt was born in 1858 in Lakeville, Dakota County, Minnesota. Her immigrant parents, James and Bridget (née Moran) Devitt, lived in Ireland during a period of privation remembered as the "darkest of years." From 1845 to 1852, an unrelenting and pervasive blight infected Ireland's potato crops and led to devastating food shortages, famine, fever, disease, extreme poverty and mass death. In 1847, known as the "Black '47," an estimated one million people died in the country and some one million more fled the country. Among them were the Devitt family, who envisioned America as a land of opportunity.

Gleaning from Jody Tesch Sorenson's multilayered and captivating book *Queen of the Desert*, the Devitt family endured an arduous month-long sea voyage.[51] Upon reaching Boston, they moved on to Chicago for a while and eventually staked their future on improving free land (akin to homesteading) in the Midwest, farming and raising cattle. They were an industrious couple whose stewardship was successful. But working the unrelenting acreage in Lakeville Township for over fifteen years took its toll.

Pulling up again in the 1870s, they traveled overland by wagon to resettle on a much smaller parcel of land outside Fargo. When most of the Devitt children were grown and out on their own, the couple then traded their hard-earned livelihood for investing in and managing an inn. James, a hearty man, enjoyed the camaraderie of entertaining hotel guests. But having borne ten children over the years while caught up in time-driven husbandry, Bridget was played out.

In this otherwise tight-knit family, there may have been a lack of sharing personal thoughts and emotions, such as women's issues. Did the Devitt women discuss Bridget's languid condition? Several years later, did they help seek solutions for Mary Alice's imminent dilemma? Had she even told them? Had marrying outside of the Catholic faith ripped apart their kinship?

The Cult of Domesticity

One wonders how much—if any—of the mounting women's rights movement and its prevailing equity issues were widespread enough to grow support in rural America. In a May 21, 1880 correspondence written by social activist and philosopher Elizabeth Cady Stanton, the goals couldn't have been clearer: "Under government, woman may be robbed, by unjust legislation, of her most sacred rights, of her inheritance, earnings, children, of education, [or] of the place she may choose in the world of work....And what is a woman's weapon of defense against all this? The ballot, which gives her a voice in the laws and her rulers."[52] Of course, it was not until May 21, 1919, nearly forty years later, that the Nineteenth Amendment was signed into law.

Yet while many women tried to divest themselves of their second-class citizenry, according to *One Hundred Years toward Suffrage: An Overview*, compiled by E. Susan Barber, "Evidence from a variety of printed sources published from [1820 to 1880], including advice manuals, poetry and literature, sermons, [and] medical text reveals that Americans, in general, held highly stereotypical notions about women's and men's roles in society. Historians would later term this phenomenon 'The Cult of Domesticity.'"[53]

Even with the dichotomy of concepts, did Mary Alice recognize the burgeoning movement that may have given her guidance in solving the betrayal she endured? Would she find eventual solace in the bosom of her family? Could she have gotten a divorce? What were the legal ramifications of being the second wife of a bigamist? And most importantly, was it that—a perceived potential stigma of being bereft of husband and carrying a child—that set her on a contrary and dangerous path?

Part Two: Going It Alone

It is possible Mary Alice confided in one or two of her siblings. But if asked, none of them knew—or would say—the reasons for their sister's departure or her whereabouts. In the meantime, Mary Alice, who later became known as Maggie, assumed her mother's maiden name, becoming Mrs. Mary Moran, left home and headed to Seattle, where she worked as a milliner until she gave birth. As for her baby, family recollections in *Queen of the Desert* vary. Mary's child may have been "twins," and they may have been sent to an orphanage in one of three Catholic convents in either Seattle or Olympia and may have received continued support from a devoted mother, who, in all probability, might never have seen her child again. Leaving as Mary

C.E. Johnson, *Dorene. Photograph courtesy of the Special Collections, Merrill-Cazier Library, Utah State University.*

Alice did required courage, and change took place. It could have been exactly what she wanted.

Free of her husband's deception (if they ever did marry), the beautiful and bold Irish woman was captivated by the wildness of the West. Drawing on her strengths, she set her sights on independence and solvency. She became the agent for the sale of her body and, needing quick money, used her sexuality prominently as her calling card. Coquettish and resilient, playful and calculating, Maggie followed licentious opportunities in active mining towns and camps, where men were many and lonely and women were few.

The Red-Light District

With silver and gold mines mushrooming in what was then western Utah Territory, Virginia City, Nevada, part of the Comstock Lode was named after Canadian mine owner Henry Comstock and designated the richest silver mine in the country in 1859. The town's highly raucous red-light district was a distinct siren call from the town's two hundred prostitutes, inviting mostly single miners—and there were streams of them—who were seeking companionship. With an eye for business, Maggie plotted her way along the "money trail." She worked as a barmaid in the early hours, probably doubled her earnings as a "soiled dove" at night and always remained a step ahead to keep up with local newspapers' mining news. In great demand, she was confident, resourceful and on the move. Soliciting in one mountain camp, wagon, town or tent after another, Mary became educated on the sexual needs and desires of men, the rewards of affability within her control and the need to stay current. It's most likely that her next stop was Pioche.

Notorious Pioche

Clinging to the side of a mountain in Nevada's High Desert, the richness of silver that made the mining boomtown of Pioche produced $600,000 in 1870 and $3,600 one year later.[54] Hundreds of miners and prospectors joined hundreds more in a frenzy to reap (or lose) their riches. Unwittingly, they often staked claims that had already been staked, stoking conflicts that bled into the stormy western backbone of mining disputes, litigation and mayhem. Pioche was considered one of the wildest towns in the Silver State, festooning its reputation on an abundance of sex workers, saloons, hurdy-gurdy houses, brothels and breweries—and an abundance of violence. Guns reigned supreme, representing the law no matter how lawless the area was. For those who could not afford protection, drinks laced with poison were not unthinkable retributions.

C.E. Johnson, *A Raucous Time Could Be Had in Virginia City. Photograph courtesy of the Special Collections, Merrill-Cazier Library, Utah State University.*

According to Candice Mortenson, the former owner of the Overland Hotel and Saloon, the "frequency of murder alone made Pioche notorious."[55] Although there was never a hanging in town, Mortenson wrote that "reliable legend insists that violent deaths accounted for seventy-two graves in Boot Hill before a citizen of Pioche died of natural causes." It was a tough town with toughened prostitutes. Maggie, in pursuit of riches, moved deeper into the Utah Territory.

Part Three: Precarious Haulage

The Need For News and Speed Sows the Pony Express

In 1860, the gold rush was at its peak; the vast Utah Territory encompassed Utah and parts of Wyoming, Colorado and much of Nevada; and the Civil War was imminent. The U.S. government, fearing western secession and the region's alliance with the South, wanted to counter political unrest and bias with ongoing, up-to-date national news. The already established 1847 postal service to the Pacific Coast by overland stagecoach delivery was just too slow.

Charting a different course of transit, three western freighters, William H. Russell, Alexander Majors and William Bradford Waddell, introduced a 1,966-mile spirited transcontinental mail delivery relay system from Missouri to San Francisco with the expressed proviso of improved communication, efficiency and speed. Promising mail deliveries within ten days, they called it the Pony Express.[56]

It was a unique system of transportation that tied the East to the West and became embedded in Western culture. Some two hundred stations were built or refurbished along existing western trails. Large home stations that were used to house riders and horses were staggered every seventy-five to one hundred miles; smaller relay (or swing) stations used to switch horses appeared every ten to fifteen miles. Four hundred station keepers, assistants and stock tenders were hired. Broadsides advertised positions for youthful riders: "Wanted: Young, skinny, wiry fellows not over eighteen. Must be expert riders, willing to risk death daily. Orphans preferred."

The routes were perilous, and nerves of steel were a prerequisite. But legends were in the making when eighty young fearless men were hired on, each one weighing less than 120 pounds and able to carry 25 pounds of equipment and 20 pounds of mail on horseback. Given two revolvers and a knife for defense, they rode day and night and were paid up to $150 a month.

The isolated Fish Springs Swing Station near the steep northern side of Fish Springs Mountains was primitive but vital to every rider who came racing in at top speeds to switch horses, grab his mochilas (custom-made mail pouches) and ride on within two minutes. It was an exchange Mark Twain described as a "whiz and a hail."

The Pony Express operated from April 1860 to October 1861. When the country's coast-to-coast telegraph system was switched on, the Pony Express was shuttered—but not in the minds of the steadfast many. Its western appeal remains a compelling trek to this day.[57]

In Maggie's time, the Fish Springs Swing Station was indeed crumbling. Yet newspaper articles describing freshly discovered silver deposits in the nearby remote area and the resultant rugged mining mecca meant the booming mining district was soon teeming with over two hundred miners who were hungry for female companionship. Maggie could not help but whet her appetite. Still, she had more travel ideas—there seemed no stopping this irresistible go-getter—as she frequented numerous mountain camps and towns along the way.

Refinement in Eureka, Utah

East Utah's Tintic Mining District was destined to become one of the richest mining areas in the country for gold, silver, lead, copper and zinc. According to the National Park Service, Eureka, the "largest, progressive and prosperous camp in the district," was fated to be the center of "supply, finance and government for the Tintic mining district."[58] Eureka was also actively engaged in Tintic folklore, those colorful paranormal activities (ghosts, howls, physical attacks and such), including frolicking tales of sexual encounters.

Men and women visiting the Eureka Mine. *Photograph used with permission from the Utah State Historical Society.*

Founded in 1869 and increasing its value of output to $5 million by 1899, "Eureka contained the ingredients of a little metropolis," wrote historian Philip F. Notarianni in his book *Faith, Hope and Prosperity: The Tintic Mining District*.[59] Its incorporation meant the establishment of a "local government, with ordinances and enforcing bodies. City officers included a mayor, treasurer, recorder, and council as well as a marshal… civic organization proved essential to the general orderly and progressive way Eureka grew."[60]

It was a melting pot of diversity, with an influx of experienced miners and new immigrants from aboard, and fraternal groups and benevolent orders were quickly established, as were churches, including Lutheran, Episcopal, Baptist and Latter-day Saint congregations. "The Catholic liturgy (mass) was offered by a visiting priest from Salt Lake City until 1884, when the residents, primarily the Irish, asked for a resident priest," Notarianni wrote. By Christmas 1885, St. Patrick's Catholic Church was built.

Entrenched in this otherwise growing, civilized community, prostitution found its niche. "The marshal received a yearly compensation of $1,200 and $1 for each arrest where the costs are paid by the defendants," noted Notarianni. As you could imagine, there "were many arrests for petty crimes."

John McChrystal, General Merchandise in Eureka. *Photograph used with permission from the Utah State Historical Society.*

Sophie Rice, alias Molly Brown, was one such case. "The local Madame and her 'ladies of the night' were arrested monthly for 'maintaining a house of prostitution' or 'advertising her vocation as a prostitute,'" Notarianni wrote. Released after paying their fines, "the marshal pocketed his dollar per arrest, and the city coffers were dollars ahead."

Maggie (now Moran) thoroughly enjoyed the hustle and bustle of Eureka (an ancient Greek phrase meaning, "I have found (it)." Its cultured society, industrious mining industry and brazen opportunities were refreshingly open to her. Apparently, she remained there for several months to work before moving on.

Mining the Miners and an Unsparing Disruption

When Maggie followed the trail to the wind-swept Fish Springs Mining District's so-named Utah Mine, she settled into a rough camp with a saloon and brothel that catered to the rush of men. The thirty-two-year-old beauty was the only "fast woman" in the area. She was ecstatic and going great guns until a younger sex worker strode into the saloon. Then there was trouble.

History, hyperbole and good old elucidation-based memory weaved plausible accounts that lay bare the consequences of two brawling women struggling for control resulting in a rumble and devastating collapse. Katie Kilkowski (or Kakashi) was young, tall and beautiful. Maggie, truly a stunner, was shorter and older.[61]

Piecing together the story, when a miner walked into the saloon with a fistful of bills, the two prostitutes vied for his attention until their attempts to corral him turned into an unsparing personal rebuke between the women. With no holds barred, insults were flung, jabs were exchanged and protests, screaming, kicking and hair pulling raged unchecked. Gaping onlookers took bets. Who knows what happened to the cash-rich miner. Bruised and gasping, the women must have stood apart from each other until, suddenly, Katie grabbed a broken whiskey bottle from the bar or a table and attacked Maggie, slashing her forehead. The bottle's raw edges also broke open the bridge of Maggie's nose and dislocated its cartilage, leaving a gaping hole and a nose crestfallen. Blood, pain and wails of anguish seized Maggie as she tried and failed to right her nose. She felt faint. Katie ran out.

Someone must have carried Maggie to a back room, where she lay in unspeakable distress. As for medical care, there were no doctors, only whiskey. Who knows how she made it through that night or the following ones. In a moment of reckless savagery, Mary Alice was disfigured, with deep lesions and a crumpled face traumatized by two nostrils appearing more porcine than human. For days, the fallen woman remained in the darkened room at the back of the saloon and slowly healed. She was no longer a beauty. Making money as a prostitute was out of the question. Indeed, she was defaced, and yes, most likely, her face flummoxed potential customers. But over time, how ever one becomes reconciled to disfigurement, Maggie did, and she was determined to work again. She was so full of grit and vitality that she mustered the courage to face and abate her pain to sprightly greet and service her customers.

Depending on who said what the day after the attack—or two weeks later in another town—Katie was found dead in a well. Rumor has it, she was drunk and fell in headfirst, with no questions asked.

Part Four: Broken Maggie and Guilt-ridden Mac Laird

Some stories say "Archibald" Mac Laird was the bartender during the vicious attack. He may have felt responsible for not pulling the women apart and wanted to set things right for Maggie. But Maggie's mind was muddled. Well-cloaked in the casual demeanor of "it's all part of the job," she continued working as a barmaid but escalated her drinking until she was intoxicated and befuddled nearly every day. It's been said that this broke Laird's heart.

It's difficult to reconcile stories of drinking to oblivion with "it's all in a day's work, as the huntsman said when the lion ate him," Charles Kingsley wrote in his 1855 book, *Westward Ho!*[62] Precipitating various adaptations of what happened next, Sorenson included excerpts of historian Earl Spendlove's conceivably richly elaborated-on and sensationalized account called "The Joy of No-Nose Maggie," which first appeared in *Real West Magazine* in May 1967.[63]

Who Saved Maggie?

Family lore recollects that Mac Laird was probably in the driver's seat when the sleeping, naked and presumably hungover Maggie was shaken awake under a blue sky in a jostling buckboard headed thirty miles southeast toward the Drum Mountain Mining District. It was 1893, Maggie was thirty-six years old and, having been abducted, she was now dropped off in the low, broad, flat and rugged mining town called Joy, which was surrounded by dry land, rattlesnakes, jackrabbits and cactus.

Mac Laird may have set her up in the town's hotel, and piqued by new surroundings, Maggie's life circumstances swiftly changed. Among a bounty of lonesome miners who could have easily satisfied her coffers, Maggie's life of prostitution was, probably—but not necessarily—over. Relying on her innate survival skills and indefatigable spirit, she saw an opportunity for respectability. Calling herself Mrs. Mary Moran, Maggie went to work at the town's café.

In west-central Utah, between the Sevier Desert to the east and Whirlwind Valley to the west, the Drum Mountains (also called the Detroit Mountains to reflect the home state of one of its founders, Harry Joy) is a desert range in Juab and Millard Counties. It was mostly mined for manganese, silver, copper and gold. As luck would have it, over time, Maggie and Mac would develop a loving arrangement and discover and make use of a gurgle of spring water that flowed through the base of the mountain.

Maggie, Mac Laird and Marriage

In 1895, Mary married Mac. He was Scottish and Mormon; she was Irish and Catholic. In their marriage certificate, she used an assumed name; he lied about his age. Whether Mary was divorced from Charlie was moot.

It didn't seem to bother her, marrying outside the Catholic faith or, for practical reasons, becoming a Mormon. Mac had a rough edge and a temper. He drank too much and argued loudly. He was also a good man, congenial and genuinely quick to help others. Mary was a good match, anticipating and emulating his every behavior. Joy was to be their home, and she truly wanted to fit in.

Joy grew into a bustling town. The couple converted a long-vacated building into a supply center called Laird's Store, and in the back, set up their household. Taking on a busy life, Maggie and Mac were committed to supplying the locals with whatever was needed and products that could be counted on. They stocked goods and medical supplies for miners and the townsfolk and offered feckless and drunk miners a place to sleep it off, a destination for long-distance wagoners and a gathering place that represented the community. To supplement their earnings, the Lairds drove cattle on an open range and, at Laird Spring, sold mountain spring water that quenched thirsty sheepmen and animals. A cave nestled behind the spring was advertised, to the delight of adventurous children; it was also a cool place to store perishables.[64]

Kind-hearted and welcoming, Mary Alice, Maggie or May, took to Joy with an open mind and found her home. She was respected by all and, despite familial bouts of battle and whisky, loved by many.

The Flu Epidemic of 1918 and Mac's Demise

According to the Centers for Disease Control and Prevention (CDC), the 1918–19 influenza pandemic, an airborne virus intensified by the massive overcrowding of troops in camps during World War I, took the lives of some 675,000 individuals in the United States.

Utah was not immune. In a March 28, 1995 article in the *Deseret News*, staff writer Twila Van Leer wrote, "As it became apparent the epidemic was going to leave no Utah community untouched, local officials set down stringent rule. Stricken homes had to display large quarantine signs." Face masks were provided by the health department and "were to be worn in the sick room and when in public. Streetcar conductors were instructed to limit the number of riders. Stores couldn't hold sales, and funeral services were [first] limited to half hour," then to mere minutes.

In the same article, Twila Peck, who grew up in the Tintic Mining District, recalled an outbreak when her father, stricken with influenza, was nursed back to life by her mother. She also remembered seeing into a neighbor's living room, where "a young mother with her infant, [were] both 'laid' out, awaiting burial."

In 1917, Mac Laird joined the many who succumbed to the flu, leaving his wife acreage and several mines. After more than two decades, Maggie, again alone, worked the store, including the addition and continuation of a U.S. post office, which had once been in her husband's charge. She built friendships, welcomed children, became a beloved "aunt" to some and tenaciously grappled with changes.

Deliverance

In 1930, Maggie saved the life of a dear friend, a sheep man, who was caught in a sudden snowstorm on horseback and appeared at her front door near to freezing. Sensing his presence—there was no knock at the door—she bolted out and ran into the storm. She then pulled the unresponsive man off his horse and chafed him with snow until he came to. Dragging him into the house, she warmed him to life by the cast iron stove.

An Act of Reunion

Although Maggie was lost to the Devitt family, she was not forgotten. Over the years, Maggie's brother Andrew came to the fore to help. When she was widowed, he brought his family, teamed up with her in the store and made up for lost time.

PART FIVE: A FINAL BETRAYAL

Just when one thinks things were going well, in 1934, a young couple who were passing through Joy met Maggie and complained about having car trouble. After being invited into Maggie's home, they viciously turned on her. They stole her possessions and money, savagely beat her and left her for dead. Maggie lay on the bare floor, more dead than alive, when a dear friend who was wondering why the store was closed ventured in and found her. After a stint in a hospital, Maggie was taken in by a caring family, who kept her safe during her final days.

Change

By December 1934, Mary Alice, a former prostitute who withstood many risky trials in her life, had become a fine and respected community member. Both she and her husband were designated in perpetuity: he as "Mount Laird" in one of the summits in Juab County located in Lady Laird Peak; she died penniless.

7

A FATAL LAPSE IN JUDGEMENT

*A*s early as 1855, when William Wormer Drummond, an associate justice of the Utah Supreme Court, appointed by President Franklin Pierce, arrived in Fillmore, the former capital of the Utah Territory (1851–56), prostitution was already an up-and-coming business on the frontier and in rural settlements and early towns.

But when the judge brought his minx to court, giggling while introducing her as his wife, many thought he'd fallen off the rails. Judge Drummond met the audacious hustler Ada Carroll, whose sobriquets embraced "Pleasant Ridgeway" and "Skinny Ada," while trolling the fleshpots of Washington, D.C.

Facts and fiction obscure when looking into Judge Drummond's times, dates and actual judicial activity. His personal transgressions are rife with rumors and kerfuffle. But from the start, the newly arrived midwesterner lied about Ada. She was not his wife. Drummond was legally married to Jemima "Ella" McClanahan. The November 21, 1888 *Chicago Inter Ocean* wrote the couple had four girls named "America, Austria, Alwilda and Bella" and one son, "Americus."

Well-educated and handsome-looking children, the girls attended school at the Convent of the Visitation. As soon as Americus celebrated his fifteenth birthday, he joined the Union army during the Civil War (1861–65). In a February 19, 1999 *Deseret News* article, staff writer Dennis Lythgoe, gleaning

C.E. Johnson, *Posing. Photograph courtesy of the Special Collections, Merrill-Cazier Library, Utah State University.*

family history from Drummond relatives, wrote that Americus joined "part of the 84th Illinois Infantry, including 850 men, 680 of whom died," and surviving was "promoted to sergeant in the Union army when the lad was only seventeen."

Drummond was known to be respectable and "fairly well-off." Born, raised and educated for the law in Virginia, he entered the legal practice in Chicago in 1851. He must have done well. A seemingly stable individual, he was mindful of his children and apparently faithful to his wife, and he was a committed member of the Democratic Party. There had to have been a drastic and sudden shift of character and rectitude for his future incomprehensible and scandalous behavior.

Was this adventuress so captivating and enchanting, the man simply flung decency to the wind without regard to its consequences? Whatever his state of mind, Drummond took to this woman and abandoned his wife and children in Oquawka, Illinois. The life he had was not one he would lead. But he was not divorced.

"Ada was said to be a 'ravishing beauty whose only physical defects were a slight lisp and a split in one of the fingers of her left hand,'" Lythgoe wrote. Sitting alongside the judge on the bench, the paramour dispensed sentencing judgments to her so-called husband. Later, there was unconfirmed hearsay that Drummond abducted two of his children.

Waywardness

Although less is known about Drummond's judicial work on the bench when he presided in Fillmore, his offenses reeked foul. In one instance, according to Lythgoe, Drummond sent his servant (or bully) named Cuffy Cato to settle a personal score with Levi Abrams, a "Mormonized Jew." Although the shopkeeper was brutally beaten, "Abrams survived the attack; and Cato and Drummond were arrested 'for assault and battery with intent to murder.'" The case was dropped. But it was no matter; the judge's reputation was sorely tarnished, his political connections twisting in "shambles."

Unbridled Loathing

Judge Drummond was an ardent antagonist of the Church of Jesus Christ of Latter-day Saints. He was convinced its members were corrupted by and more devoted to the LDS Church and President Brigham Young than they were to the United States Constitution. Vocal in his disdain, Drummond "spread numerous, vicious rumors about Brigham Young and Mormons, including charges of treason and murder," Lythgoe wrote.

Recommending President James Buchanan (1857–61) appoint a "non-Mormon in [Mr. Young's] place," Drummond's deceptive actions created a maelstrom, some critics say, that fueled Buchanan's brusque decision to send General Albert Sidney Johnston's "2,500-man military force" to escort Alfred Cummings to Utah to replace Brigham Young as territorial governor.

Called Buchanan's Blunder, according to historian Richard D. Poll, the Utah War was a "costly, disruptive, and unnecessary confrontation between the Mormon people in Utah Territory and the government and army of the United States. It resulted from misunderstandings that transformed a simple decision to give Utah Territory a new governor into a year-long comedy of errors with a tragic potential."[65]

Interpreted as religious persecution, it caused many Mormons to leave their homes and belongings. Brigham Young asserted that the judge should be stripped of his post. In Lythgoe's *Deseret News* article titled "Utah's Rogue Judge," Mr. Young called Drummond "a dog or wolf, vicious and brutal, whining, and snappish, vain as a peacock and ignorant as a jackass."

Free Fall

Erstwhile, in 1857, Judge Drummond sold tomes of his law books to Hosea Stout, a complicated, controversial and leading figure in the LDS Church. The sales transaction might have been done to lighten the judge's load or to make him enough money to plan a move. The judge and his lady then traveled to Carson Valley (and Nevada's first town) in the Utah Territory, ostensibly to hold court. "But secretly," the *Deseret News* journalist wrote, the couple "intended to leave Utah for the East via California and the Isthmus of Panama."

That same year, Drummond wrote a scathing resignation letter to the Honorable Jeremiah S. Black, attorney general of the United States, which was reprinted in the April 14, 1857 *New York Daily Times*. Listing by number every issue, complaint, example and reason for surrendering his post, Drummond accused "Brigham Young as the 'vicegerent' of God and prophetic successor of Joseph Smith, who was the founder of this blind and treasonable organization." Then in 1860, with his mistress in tow, Drummond returned to a law practice in Chicago. But obviously, his reputation was so sullied that he was in free fall.

Skinny Ada was well known in the Chicago area. The *Chicago Inter Ocean* exposed her as having been similarly involved with a congressman from Illinois, with liaisons "almost as notorious as that with Drummond."

For whatever reason, the jewel-eyed harlot was not done with Drummond. "[Pleasant Ridgeway] eventually dragged him down as was herself and left him to sink lower," the *Chicago Inter Ocean* alleged. "And then things went from bad to worse." Unceremoniously dropping the judge, Ada took up with an unscrupulous bird dealer.

Drummond "dabbled in doubtful practices of various kinds and was finally disbarred from legal practice." No longer working and constantly drinking, Drummond moved from one cheap lodging to other cheap rooms in the rough parts of town. Former friends, doubtful of his words, stayed away. He shared rent and associated with petty criminals, his knowledge of the law possibly advising them.

"Arrested for stealing letters from mailboxes on street corners," Drummond continued drinking even when one of his daughters stepped in to help with money, food, clothing and friendship. Despite her efforts, she was unsuccessful, and Drummond continued to drink.

The once-brilliant man, now a habitual drunkard, fell from grace. On November 20, 1888, his dead body was discovered slumped over in a near-pitch-black corner of a lonely, lowly grog house.

8

COAL CAMPS, RAILS, TOWNS AND WOMEN

GREEN RIVER

Surrounded by desert mountains known as the Book Cliffs in eastern Utah, Green River was settled by non-Mormons in the late 1870s. Once considered "valueless," unfarmable land, the region's meandering, fordable river and looming, sequence stratification range that begins near Helper, Utah, and extends to Grand Junction, Colorado, soon made it a force of its own and outstanding as a major crossroad in the West. Contrary to popular belief, Green River's sandy soil reaped an agricultural bounty of national distinction for its impeccable peaches and its vast varieties of enormously sweet plums and juicy melons.

In 1880, Green River was a boomtown, with a surge of workers arriving to construct a bridge across the river and lay a roadbed for the Denver and Rio Grande Western Railway. The railroad's completion in 1883 shifted the town's economy to shipping livestock, railroad equipment, supplies and freight, and it made Green River a home and workplace open to a diversity of people of all ethnicities, cultures, religions and traditions.

Located along the Outlaw Trial—which leads eastward from Robbers Roost in southeastern Utah to Vernal, Utah, and over to Brown's Park in Daggett County (Utah) and Moffat Country (Colorado)—Green River's mantle took on the still lived and loved Wild West reputation.

The Book Cliffs, Green River. *Photograph used with permission from the Utah State Historical Society.*

While steeped in lore, many of us know Butch Cassidy was a ranch owner, cattle rustler, horse thief, bank and train robber, former convict and captivating leader of the Wild Bunch Gang, who "broke ground on the Outlaw Trail," eschewed violence and apparently never killed a living soul.

Robert Leroy Parker, the first of thirteen siblings, was born in Beaver, Utah, in 1866. Raised by Mormon pioneer parents on the family ranch in nearby Circleville, the boy left home at twelve. He acquired his nickname, Butch, most likely from working on a chuckwagon or in a meat market in Rock Springs, Wyoming. His surname was gleaned from an esteemed cowhand and small-time cattle rustler named Mike Cassidy.

Traveling throughout the West and purchasing a small ranch in Johnson County, Wyoming, Butch Cassidy wrangled with cattle barons over grazing land and water rights and was heralded as a warrior rather than a villain. By 1880, he was well launched on his descent into crime.

The Butch Cassidy Five (studio shot). *Photograph used with permission from the Uintah County Library Regional History Center, all rights reserved.*

MATT WARNER

"It—Butch's misdeeds—had to do with outlaw Matt Warner, who showed Parker and his two brothers, Daniel and Arthur, the ropes on robbing the Moffat Bank in Denver, Colorado, and the Telluride Bank with his brother-in-law Tom McCarty," said documentary filmmaker and writer Dr. Steve Lacy in several conversations with this author in mid-December 2022.

Called the Mormon Kid, Matt Warner was born Willard Eratus Christiansen to Mormon parents. He became a bank robber, cattle rustler, rancher, ferryman, bootlegger and convict. After being sentenced to five years in the Utah Territorial Prison and pardoned early due to good behavior, the Mormon Kid was temporarily honest. He mended his ways, later becoming a justice of the peace and eventually the sheriff of Price. Around 1887, Warner owned and operated a bar and brothel in Green River. As Dr. Lacy tells it:

The brothel was a two-story wooden building with indoor plumbing. It also had a bathroom on the second floor. There were no electric lights, but kerosene lamps were used to brighten up the rooms at night and in the closet. A long, narrow window was used during the day. The four bedrooms upstairs were all smartly decorated for the anticipated activity. Each room had a brass bed, a small nightstand, a cabinet with drawers, water pitcher with bowls and towels on top of a rack....The living room was downstairs with a big pot belly stove in the middle used to heat the room, and a kitchen with a cookstove. Off to the side was a parlor, where the ladies entertained the men who came from Matt's bar or the railroad station a half block away. Then they would go upstairs for sexual transactions.

"Warner's bar, behind the brothel and a quick walk through the block, was a small affair, where they served beer, whisky, cigars and other spirits," Lacy said. "The place got so hot inside during the summer months, the customers went outside with their drinks along with regular chatter and banter—and to see how far they could spit watermelon seeds."

Dr. Lacy added that neither Butch nor Sundance (Harry Alonzo Longabaugh) indulged in the women's services. "The only female Butch spent time with was his wife, Lena," Lacy said. Sundance may have been married to his consort Etta Place, who was rumored to have been a prostitute

Matt Warner's brothel in Green River.
Photograph courtesy of Dr. Steven Lacy.

Above: Harry Alonzo Longabaugh, also known as the Sundance Kid, and Butch Cassidy (Robert Leroy Parker) outside Watt Warner's Saloon in Green River. *Photograph used with permission from the Utah State Historical Society.*

Left: The Sundance Kid with Etta Place, Bliss Bros Photography, 368 Main Street, Buffalo, New York. *Photograph courtesy of the Library of Congress.*

Right: An outlaw and gunman in Butch Cassidy's gang, Kid Curry (Harvey Logan), with a prostitute. *Photograph used with permission from the Utah State Historical Society.*

Below: Unidentified prostitutes in a brothel. *Photograph courtesy of Dr. Steven Lacy.*

Above: Unidentified prostitutes in a brothel. *Photograph courtesy of Dr. Steven Lacy.*

Opposite: Price, Utah Castle Valley, Coal Co. coal train. *Photograph used with permission from the Utah State Historical Society.*

and known as an outlaw. "But," Lacy said, "both men used the brothel as they would a hotel." Perhaps they were the only two who did.

In 1900, according to Lacy, Butch Cassidy's uncle Daniel Gillies bought the brothel from Matt. His family lived in it, and when Gillies died in 1907, his family resided there until 1994.

Today, Matt's abandoned brothel is owned by Dr. Lacy.

PRICE, UTAH

By 1883, the coal industry and the expansion of the railroad dramatically changed the city of Price from an agrarian community to a commercial hub. Thousands of foreign-born non-Mormons, including Italian, Greek, Eastern European, Japanese and Austrian immigrants flooded to the area to work for the railroad or in the mines, defining Price, the county seat of Carbon County (and part of Emery County in 1892), as an ethnically rich, refreshingly complex and diverse cultural hub.

Price in 1890. *Photograph used with permission from the Utah State Historical Society.*

J. Bracken Lee. *Photograph used with permission from the Utah State Historical Society.*

"Along with a number of churches, movie theaters and one theater that offered live performances, boxing and weddings, there was some illegal gambling done in the basement of the Savoy Hotel, with prostitutes in the upper rooms," Lacy explained. "This brothel was not as elegant as most other whorehouses of this period."

When J. Bracken Lee, who was not a member of the LDS Church, jumpstarted his political career as mayor of Price in 1935, Lacy said his leniency on alcohol (Price had become an open city), gambling and prostitution was not without controversy:

> *In 1936, when he was sworn in, J. Bracken Lee's first act was to move prostitutes off the streets. "I cleaned it up," he said. "[The women] moved to two different hotels, including the Savoy, and [we] made them take weekly medical tests from the doctor." The mayor—he was known as "Brack"—went on to say he sold life insurance to two of the madams.*

From 1949 to 1957, J. Bracken Lee served two terms as the governor of Utah, six two-year terms as the mayor of Price and three terms as the mayor of Salt Lake (1960–72). He was described as a confident and compelling maverick, and the October 21, 1966 *Deseret News*, wrote that "Lee once uttered the words that made him famous, 'Do it honestly, do the best you know how, and let 'em holler!'" And surely they did!

Helper

Seven miles northwest of Price, flanked on one side by the rugged Book Cliffs and known as the coalfield "Hub of Carbon County," the mining and railroad town of Helper was named for helper locomotives that assisted freight trains in making the steep climb up Soldier Summit at 7,477 feet.

Historian Philip F. Notarianni said that in the 1900s, Helper was also home to sixteen different nationalities, including Italians, Finns, Austrians, Chinese, Greeks, Southern Slavs and Japanese, who "represented merchants and laborers [and] influenced the town's social landscape."[66]

Helper flourished with enclaves of vibrant and varied traditions, religions, beliefs, folk medicines, tales "and customs representing products of cultural distinctiveness," Notarianni added.

Its street life, too, was enlivened with bars, pool halls, coffeeshops and a steady stream of customers who, according to Roman Vega, director

Main Street in Helper, circa 1908. *Photograph used with permission from the Utah State Historical Society.*

Crossing the divide at Soldier Summit, 1910. A four header and one rear helper. *Photograph used with permission from the Utah State Historical Society.*

Lizzett's Store depot in Helper (postcard, 1886). *Photograph used with permission from the Utah State Historical Society.*

of Helper's Western Mining and Railroad Museum, flocked to any one of the five brothels reserved on the second floor of hotels, as well as the gambling clubs in the back rooms of businesses straddling downtown Helper's Main Street.

While plentiful prostitutes raked through the numerous nearby and busy coal camps, such as those in Spring Canyon, ladies of the night regularly serviced the many mostly single, lonely men in the hotels. For those who found their way to the bordello in the Carbon Hotel and walked up to the second floor, there was no way to get around the short, Black madam with red hair and freckles.

If admitted, Sister Babe (Utah-born Anna Patterson), who also acted as a bouncer, insisted customers wash themselves with soap and water before participating in a sexual act. The hotel sported about eleven mostly identical rooms. Customers found a wash basin (and, later, a small sink) with clean towels on the left side of the small room; the bed was in the middle, and against the other wall was a dresser with candles on top.

"Sister Babe wanted clean, healthy girls and every month would take them to Chuck's Pharmacy on Main Street to have them checked out," Vega explained. "She, like most of the madams, contributed to the city, paid their fines and helped support children causes."

Left, top: Second-floor cribs at the Helper Hotel in Helper. *Photograph courtesy of the Helper's Mining and Railroad Museum.*

Left, bottom: The Rio Hotel, one of the five hotels with cribs on the second floor. *Photograph courtesy of the Helper's Mining and Railroad Museum.*

Opposite, top left: Sister Babe (Anne Peterson), madam. *Photograph courtesy of the Helper's Mining and Railroad Museum.*

Opposite, top right: A Helper prostitute. *Photograph courtesy of the Helper's Mining and Railroad Museum.*

Opposite, bottom: A prostitute's room exhibit at the Helper Museum. *Photograph courtesy of the Helper's Mining and Railroad Museum.*

There were no street walkers in the town. Working girls lived in the hotels, brothels and bordellos. And because of their economic significance to Helper and the enormous number of miners who came to town, they were accepted in the community.

Dr. Lacy remembered a family story—whether true or fanciful—that was repeated in numerous remembrances of others in rural towns throughout Utah:

> *There were four Carbon High School boys looking for excitement in Helper. They heard that* [one of the brothels] *was the place to go. Didn't think it was going to cost much. Come to find out, they had to pool their money, all of five dollars, which all went to the oldest. Out of money, the other three were too embarrassed to ever try again. At least, that's what I heard. Years later, the girls in Helper were on a circuit where they rotated the ladies from Nevada and Utah so there would be fresh girls all the time.*

A corner exhibit of a prostitute's room. *Photograph courtesy of the Helper's Mining and Railroad Museum.*

By the early 1970s, with a new police chief in town, prostitution, which had always been illegal, was shut down—maybe. As for the presence of tunnels and tales of nefarious activities that took place under Main Street, Vega hasn't yet found any old city (sewer) map drawings to sustain their existence. "Nothing was shown of any tunnels," he said—but gives a nod to the locals and what they thoroughly know and have to say.

9

THE MADAM, THE BOARDER AND THE COOK

PART ONE: THE BROTHEL KEEPER'S DILEMMA

The Nutshell Game

Since prostitution has long been considered the oldest profession in the world, one wonders whether it and its onus bear resemblance to the old shell game: the thimblerig, the four shells and a pea or three and a walnut, coin, bottle cap or token. Many consider it a controlled and swift con game achieved by a sharp, swindling trickster's sleight of hand and the skill of a shill whose consistent wins entice potential flats (or victims) who are too hungry to heed common sense or, pondering the consequences, can't resist the thrill of the gamble.

In a nutshell, never more so in the risky and repeatedly unsafe world of the frail prostitute does the phrase "you win some; you lose some" supplant the walnut and pea than in a courtroom scene, where cultured legalese battles the unbridled performance of an experienced prostitute who can sum up a john within seconds. It could also show up as a loss when the curious relationship between hooker and police becomes risky and sets the pea on edge or, for that matter, when monthly fines control the game as morality wrestles with the "necessary evil" rationale of city fathers who look to those who work on their backs to fatten their civic coffers.

C.E. Johnson, *Modele dans L'Atelier*. *Photograph courtesy of the Special Collections, Merrill-Cazier Library, Utah State University.*

Elsie St. Omar, the Madam

Take the case of Salt Lake City's Elsie St. Omar (née Anderson) and her fledglings, who found themselves at predictable odds with the law. Recording the Salt Lake Police Court's recent activity, the August 23, 1890 *Salt Lake Tribune* wrote that city patrolmen raided "four joints where men [who are] not over-scrupulous as to their morals, can drive dull care away. The first nest, most emptied of its birds, was Elsie St. Omar's, back of Commercial Street," reported the paper. "It was she who opened the house a few weeks ago, for which printed invitations were sent out and responded to largely."

The *Salt Lake Tribune* described the brothel owner, Elsie St. Omar, as a "stylish, handsome-looking girl [who] would hardly shine as a missionary to 'Corea'" and posed that law enforcement was ardent in its efforts to "root out the harlots" from the city's respectable, primarily white residential homes. In short order, St. Omar, known as a keeper, was arrested along with inmates of the house Sadie Ray, Mary Hart, Vera Steyer and Cora Burtons. Pleading guilty, the madam was fined fifty dollars and each inmate twenty-five dollars, and after paying, were all released.

Later that same night on West Third South Street, May Sinclair and her two associates, Sadie Johnson and Newman, were "wafted in" and released only after forfeiting fines of fifty dollars and twenty-five dollars, respectively. A West Temple nymph called Kitty was also pulled in with her partner in crime Rose Wilson, while a West Side pullet and her companion chicken, May Stewart, a known "inmate of the roost," paid similar fines. Few surprises were had.

It occurred to some that seizing sex-selling transgressors not only created a financial boost for the city but also eased into a normal work pattern for street police. Moreover, it served well as a reminder to novice prostitutes not to gamble on a shell game that was anything but a sure thing—as was exemplified in the chaotic summer of 1892.

Days of Entanglement: Law, Sex and Inequity

On June 13, 1892, Mrs. Maggie Kirk, who emanated respectability in society, was arrested for "conducting an assignation house, along with the worst kind of opium joint," the *Salt Lake City Herald-Republican* reported. Charged and fined twenty-five dollars, Maggie was sent to the city jail for ninety days.

Four days later, on June 17, during a purportedly placid evening among the denizens, Elsie's brothel was shaken up by a surprise drop-in and unorthodox assemblage of city councilmen, police, Salt Lake City newspaper men, one judge and a self-appointed detective. Gathering for a walk-about to investigate brothels, these men ostensibly showed up to interview the brothel's occupants. They overstayed their welcome, and despite any reasonable intent, their actions may have triggered an investigation into police impropriety, none of which was brought out in a courtroom.

Elsie St. Omar was arrested again on a warrant charging her with keeping a house of ill fame. The brothel keeper, her boarder Rose Miller and her

109

cook Goldie Shears were each fined a one-hundred-dollar bond. Elsie could not justify that amount and, on June 21, stood before the Salt Lake City justice of the peace Fred Kesler, prepared to contradict the order.

"I have reason to believe and do believe that I cannot have a fair and impartial trial before the said Fred Kesler, before whom this case is now called for trial, by reason of the prejudice and bias of said justice," read Elsie in a statement subscribed and sworn to before a notary public.[67]

Miss St. Omar claimed the fixed fines of one hundred dollars each for her (the madam), Rose Miller (a boarder) and Goldie Shears (the cook) were requested by arresting officers Joseph E. O'Brien and George A. Sheets, who was also the complaining witness. She alleged on that same night, the said justice charged Hattie Wilson, convicted several times during the past year, and Lucy Andrews fifty dollars each for keeping a house of ill repute. Later, other Salt Lake City prostitutes, including May Smith, Kitty Wilson, Maud Mitchell, Dora Hansen and Grace Johnson, were each fined fifty dollars. Only the bonds of St. Omar, Miller and Shears were doubled.

"It is the duty of the city attorney to prosecute and defend in all courts in all actions on behalf of the city," the steadfast, self-assured and appealing St. Omar paraphrased from an 1892 Salt Lake City ordinance.[68]

Although the complaint was filed on June 20, St. Omar maintained Justice Fred Kesler and George Sheets did not immediately report such facts to the city attorney E.D. Hoge or his deputy and prosecuting attorney E.F. Coad. "The first information [Mr. Coad] had concerning the matter was on the morning of the 23rd, when he saw an account of my arrest in the morning paper," Elsie said. Calling Kesler a material witness, who heard of and acquiesced to the request of one-hundred-dollar bonds from witnesses for the prosecution, the brothel owner cautioned she would subpoena the justice to show the "malice and animus of the prosecution." She demanded the trial case be moved to another venue with jurisdiction and that the bail for each of the three women be reduced. This was denied. The women's problems were far from over; a court date was set.

Sensing a scandalous melodrama that would last for days, by ten o'clock on the morning of June 25, the courtroom of onlookers, lawyers and newspaper reporters churned to overflowing as they jostled to catch sight of the curvaceous St. Omar and her chickens. Many anticipated the madam-boarder-cook conundrum would be both entertaining and exposed. One could only imagine the howls that erupted when they were so profoundly disappointed by the defendants' attorney, Mr. D.C. Eichnor, suddenly withdrawing from the case. (Questions had been raised about the propriety of his counsel, as he was also holding the office of assistant county attorney.) Unacquainted with the case, attorney D.N. Straup stepped in for the defendants.

Along with the straightforward complaint by Miss St. Omar, other grievances surfaced: the inference that someone was imitating an officer and the unsettling question of legality regarding warrants and fines. Tossed into rebuttals, the case promised to be both strategic and thorny.

Presented before Justice Fred Kesler, St. Omar's trial was slated to continue the following day. Immediately, the defense counsel strove to quell the warrant issue and all its proceedings. Mr. Straup claimed they were "defective, illegal and void," the June 28, 1892 *Salt Lake Tribune* reported in "Uncovering of a Good Deal of Rottenness Begun."

A day earlier, under the June 27 *Salt Lake Times*'s headline, "A Sensational Turn," much was made of officer Joe E. O'Brien, who, as a private citizen, did not go through the proper channels that required the signature of the current mayor, R.N. Baskin, and a member of the Utah Liberal Party. Nor did the recommendation take place within the stated ten-day cycle, in which time, O'Brien's nomination would have qualified for such a position.

Considering the defendant had not been properly served and that the offense was, at most, a misdemeanor, Mr. Straup objected. It didn't matter. A verbal brouhaha frayed the air. The court intervened. The trial was launched, and the witnesses came forth.

Avoiding questions about his profession (although he was never asked), O'Brien denied any wrongdoing or attachment in the matter. But he said he had been told St. Omar kept a house of prostitution.

A prostitute named Marian Fields testified that she (and others) had lived and worked in Elsie St. Omar's houses. Described as a "hatched-faced soiled dove," Fields, the *Salt Lake Tribune* reported, spoke of a trunk held in the house in lieu of an unpaid bill, and a sign that said "Furnished Rooms" posted in the window. Of course, pitting prostitute against prostitute, somebody inevitably loses. It may have been a precarious move for Fields. Against St. Omar from the get-go, Fields might have been jealous of the madam's business. Unreconciled to her status as a prostitute, working in a house rather than running the house, she might have had an ulterior get-ahead motive.

Officer Sheets recalled Elsie's reputation as an "unsavory character." He had seen hacks approaching the house and men leaving at 2:00 a.m. He knew well of her appearances in court, but he was not, he said, an expert and was unable to find any evidence to arrest her.

Officer Sullivan, too, had seen men coming and going from the house. One night, Elsie opened the door to let him in, yelling, "Ladies, come into the parlor!" "And they came," he said.

A.M. Wilson testified that on the night of Elsie's arrest, he saw several men jump out a window and climb over the fence "in their eagerness to get away." He did not arrest them because he hadn't a warrant for them. Officer Sullivan concurred: four men, one carrying a coat, and a woman, who had temporarily escaped before being caught.

Mr. Straup posed the men were "simply roomers at the house, frightened by the disturbance." He asked about the screens over the windows: "Maybe [the screens are in] now, but [they weren't] then," one officer replied.

If there was no doubt about why they were there, Coad questioned, "Why weren't they arrested?"

"If they were not guilty, why did they run?" an officer fired back.

The Prosecution Rested. The Defense Opened.

As the audience gawked, captivated by the unruffled and composed buxom Elsie, a slew of witnesses came forward in her defense. Her next door neighbor W.D. Palmer said that, from time to time, he furnished St. Omar with carriages and believed the woman's reputation for "morals and charity" was good. A grocer knew of Elsie's past and claimed she had reformed and was engaged to be married. A stone cutter, who worked on the Eighth Ward Square occasionally, rented one of Elsie's rooms and had nothing to say because he was seldom there.

The blacksmith at 219 Fourth South Street heard a rumor, but beyond that, he had nothing else to add. Another boarder named George E. McErlin denied ever telling anyone that St. Omar was "running a house of prostitution on the quiet." The saloon keeper on 373 State Street "knew nothing about Elsie, never went there and never wanted to."

Hugh L. Glenn's testimony generated interest. A deputy United States marshal who had left the police force, Glenn passed Elsie's house nearly every evening "but never saw anything wrong," the *Salt Lake Tribune* reported. The marshal did remember hearing a masculine voice one time call to Elsie from the porch, inquiring if he could visit her. She shouted back, "I am not running a house now and cannot let you in."

Hugh Glenn often visited St. Omar's house. In June, when asked to make an arrest, he joined a party of city officials, street supervisors and reporters.

When the prosecutor Mr. Coad asked if the marshal was "using every effort to hinder the officers in the presence of their duties since he had left the force," Glenn replied he was "trying to show up some of their work." (There was no clarification of the "work" that was done, and later, Glenn's occupation as a deputy U.S. marshal was rebutted.)

When asked if he had considerable feeling toward the defendant, Glenn answered that he had "feelings against any persecution." One had to wonder then where the case was going. Objecting to the bushwhacking line of questioning, one terse question following another, Mr. Straup was overruled but not discouraged.

The Cook

Goldie Shears was anxious and maybe even cowed by the court's and spectators' attention. When asked if St. Omar's house illegally sold beer, Goldie Shears replied no and, speaking in her defense, alluded to her father, who had long abandoned the family, and her mother, who died and left Goldie on her own. Feeling defenseless and often wronged by others, she stretched to make ends meet and found herself at odds with the sex trade. It's true that for a few years, she did hustle as a prostitute. But now, she worked for Elsie St. Omar as a cook and was paid four dollars a week. Distracted on the day she heard an arrest was in the works, she left the house to get change for a "five-dollar bill"—for whom, we don't know—and was caught by one of the officers descending on the house. She told the court there were no wrongdoings at the house.

The Madam

Taking the stand, Miss St. Omar said, yes, she had kept a house of prostitution but was no longer in the business. Expecting her mother and sister to arrive for a visit, she rented a private home with the strong desire that her relatives would know nothing about her past ventures.

She answered no when the prosecutor asked if one man's clothes had been found in a chamber that was not the room he rented as a boarder; no, when asked if the clothes of a woman were found in a room occupied by two men; and no, she never sold beer in the house, not even during the councilmen's visit, "when she sent out to get it."

Casual consensus was in accord that St. Omar ran brothels, including her latest Commercial Street rental venue, although no clients or rowdies were to be found or coaxed to be called upon to give testimony. There was no male customer willing to say he paid to engage in sex with a sporting lady.

No one was caught engaging in illegal sexual activities (which would warrant an arrest), and while there was stirring jockeying between lawyers and severity in court decisions, no revelations or tempestuous scandals were divulged in any depth to titillate the large, crowded courtroom—other than those enthralled by looking at how she carried herself and her appearance, style of speech and confident attitude.

The question of warrants—regardless of the legality of the server—did remain suspect; and whether St. Omar was a clever enough liar who spoke with resolve, she was steadfast in her innocence.

This potentially cut-and-dried court case carried an aura incongruous with the allegations against St. Omar, Miller and Shear. What exactly were the subtle inferences in the court case cached under a walnut shell?

Before the day's end, Elsie was found guilty of running a house of ill fame, and her fate was to be decided on the following morning, after Rose, who was ready to fight, testified.

Part Two: A Woman Bothered

A Scandal-Peppered Background

Rose Miller was bothered. She was bothered by the actions of several officers, like Officer Matthews, who offered her his gold ring, vowing to stay only with her, but refused to pay for her services. She gave him back his ring. She was bothered by another unnamed officer who obsessively pursued her. But it was Officer George Albright who worried her the most, as he insisted, she said, that she was his girl. When she refused, he became possessive, moody and threatening, and of course, he carried a gun, which frightened her more. In mid-June, Rose called on city council members for help.

"[Rose] is the girl who says Officer Albright has been persecuting her and who threatened to kill her just before he left the city with [a] crowd for Chicago," the June 23, 1892 *Salt Lake Herald-Republican* theorized. "The fact that the girls were [hauled] in so soon after making the affidavit against Albright gives a very suspicious cast to the entire proceeding."

The Taste of Indignity

On the next day of St. Omar's trial, fueled by rumors of misconduct and a flurry of activity among members of the police force, onlookers packed the courtroom. Rose Miller was again put on the stand. Not knowing who purchased the beer at Elsie's home during the councilmen's visit, Rose briefly touched on her difficulties with specific officers, Mr. O'Brien and Officers Sheets and Matthews. The men rejected her accusations.[69]

The two men denied saying they would "run Elsie out of town." Mr. O'Brien contended he certainly didn't remember saying that and said that if he had indeed done so, he was only joking.

According to the June 29, 1892 *Salt Lake Herald-Republican*, Rose heard both men express that sentiment about Elsie—and more. "When Elsie stopped to speak to the boy who takes care of her horse, Sheets said, 'Quit that monkeying around, or I will call the cart and put you in it!'" Scolding them all the way to city hall, "they threatened to put us behind bars, and one of them said, "We'll show you that you haven't George Albright to deal with."

While they waited for bail, Rose said that they were "jammed against the wall, dragged off and shoved into a dirty cell," with the admonition they were no better than the others who were held there.

When the prosecutor Coad asked if Rose called the officer a "long-legged so-and-so" after she heard that Sheets had sworn to the complaint, she replied she hadn't. Elsie, recalled to the stand, testified she never heard anyone make a comment like that to Sheets, nor did she ever use such language. Matthews swore he had never been in the house, except in the line of duty. According to the *Salt Lake Tribune*, "He denied positively ever wanting to be [Rose's] lover," ever relinquishing his ring, or "ever making such a suggestion to her." A hack driver who accompanied Officer Matthews to collect a back bill for Rose said that when she paid the bill, she swore about "getting even with Matthews."

Part Three: What Just Happened?

Claims Made

Between the lawyers' not-so-good-humored raillery during the trial and the lingering unexposed quagmire underfoot—although newspapers' lurid accounts were expressive and current—the closing arguments were surprisingly brief.

Speaking for the defense, Mr. Straup argued that if Elsie's house was one of prostitution, "why is it that not one person in the neighborhood would testify to that fact?" He also acknowledged the nagging suspicion of bitterness swamping the court trial. "He didn't want to impute bad motives to any officer," the *Salt Lake Tribune* conveyed, "but did think they exhibited more than usual interest on the case."

Mr. Straup asked for a dismissal.

The prosecutor Mr. Coad maintained there was no such persecution, that the defense was out to "injure the police force" and took advantage of the officers who went to the house in their line of duty. "I have no feeling in this case, except to see the law vindicated. All the animus has been shown by the defense," he concluded.

The Court Determines

According to the *Salt Lake Tribune*, in giving a decision, the judge declared, "This case is one of those classes of crime done with doors closed, [and] the only way to prove the defense, generally, is by reputation. A great deal of testimony, which had no [specific] bearing on the case, was taken," he added. "I shall confine myself to the testimony as to the reputation of the house. The duty of the policemen is to protect the good order of the city. These men come here and are sworn to tell the truth. And the court had no right to disbelieve them. They testify positively that the reputation of the house is that it's a house of prostitution."

Elsie was fined one hundred dollars and Rose fifty dollars; Goldie was released for lack of evidence. Mr. Straup vowed to take the case to the third district court.

A Trio: Moving Out, Reinventing Oneself or Staying

Nary a word remains of what happened to Goldie and whether she was a cook or a chicken.

Months later, calling Rose Miller a "somewhat famous belle of the demimonde of this city," the August 24, 1893 *Salt Lake Tribune* explained that her house on West Third South Street was raided. Charged by Captain Donovan, Rose was reckless. She offered the captain a $5 tip to, one, make it more "interesting" and, two, "say nothing about the incident." When that didn't work—"his record was above reproach"—she tried blackmailing him in a muddle of tales equating stolen rubies and diamonds and inferring his part in the robbery. Captain Donovan didn't bite, the paper informed readers. Rose eventually withdrew her accusation saying it was only a passing rumor. Her bonds were set at $50 for running a brothel and $250 for the charge of blackmail.

Did this trial abolish the lucrative business Elsie St. Omar once had and said she was leaving? Remaining in business, paying fines, showing up in court, suddenly leaving town and silently returning, often changing one's name, location or story, can be an exhausting endeavor for anyone. But being well-seasoned in the caprices of politics and legal proceedings, Elsie St. Omar stayed the course. She didn't gamble on a shell game that was not under her control. And she didn't flee.

No doubt, Elsie continued doing what she did best: selling sex.

Eight Years Later

On October 19, 1901, the *Salt Lake Herald-Republican* reported a fifteen-year-old went missing from her home, triggering a two-week frantic search by her parents that was expanded on by other relatives until, at their wit's end, they called the police.

Within a day or two, an officer saw "the girl entering the resort of Elsie St. Omar on Commercial Street and, recognizing her from [her parents' description], followed her into the place." Before the teen had a chance to hide, the officer took her into custody and then safeguarded her home to her mother. "The girl offered no resistance," the paper recounted. "It is said [she] seemed to be entirely unconcerned about her conduct."

The teenager mentioned a woman named Myrtle led her toward the house. Allegedly having no idea the destination was a house of prostitution, the girl was somewhat encouraged (or perhaps tempted) to stay. The proprietress of the resort, Elsie St. Omar, acknowledged the girl's two-week residency. She affirmed the runaway expressed a desire to stay and represented herself to be of age.

Infallible

A year later, in an August 28, 1902 *Salt Lake Herald Republican* special report, it was said a fire broke out in a nine-room dwelling on the outskirts of Silver

City, a silver boomtown near Eureka, Utah, in the heart of the Tintic Mining District. Elsie St. Omar owned the building that one might call a resort. The structure and its belonging were gutted. Miss St. Omar carried an insurance policy. The inmates were presumably working in Eureka at the time, and the cause of the fire remained unknown.

Part Four: Including the Elephant That Wasn't in the Court Room

Revisiting Rose

What about the investigation that shadowed the court trial and had many all atwitter?

The June 18, 1892 *Deseret Evening News* headline, "The Frail Female Who Is Afraid of Being Killed by Policeman," was buttressed by "Woman's Sensational Story" before devolving into "A Deplorable State of Affairs." This must have knee-jerked the attention of readers. While citing an anonymous interview for the paper told in full, the very woman and her egregious tale of mental and sexual abuse most certainly shared a compelling resemblance to the experience of Rose Miller, who spoke with reporters from the *Salt Lake Tribune* and the *Deseret Evening News* while visiting St. Omar's brothel.

"For some time, past and dark insinuations have been made in certain quarters regarding the conduct of some of the members of the city police force…with sufficient cognizance of the rumors to institute an inquiry," the *Deseret Evening News* began.

The woman, Rose, acknowledged the fact that she was a sporting girl, well known to Officer George Albright and the appellant who asked members of the city council for help when she feared for her life.

George Albright was a policeman who worked his beat in the tenderloin district, patrolling the streets. He was familiar with the area's prostitutes and brothels and had a favorite one, which crossed the line. "Some people used their authority to abuse and exploit women," author Jeffrey Nichols wrote.[70] Officer Albright instinctively knew the vulnerability and insecurity that daily beset prostitutes and allegedly used their weaknesses for his pleasure.

Albright wasn't alone. Salt Lake City's Captain William B. Parker was considered by his own men to be punitive, aggressive and, it turns out, unstable. When several working women and members of the police force reproached him for his violent nature, Parker was demoted by the council, "apparently as a backdoor means of removing him," Nichols wrote. Parker believed Albright was one of his accusers. He tracked him down and pulled out his gun to shoot. It misfired. Officer Albright shot Parker dead. It was an act of self-defense.

Trouble

Months before moving to St. Omar's, the *Deseret Evening News* clarified, Rose worked in brothels run by Sadie Noble and Minnie Barton. It was there she met Officer Albright, who soon spoke of his affection and love for her. "He wanted me to be his 'girl' and insisted I go to his room and live with him," Rose said. "This I refused to do, [but] he came to see me often and continued to force his company upon me."

It is possible Rose believed being in a physical relationship with a cop would have some guaranteed protection. She was mistaken. In her line of business, it would be difficult for Rose to say she had been sexually molested and be taken seriously. Rose begged Albright to stay away from her, which only strengthened his resolve and heightened her fear. She sought to pacify him and diffuse his erratic behavior, and to accomplish this, she said she submitted to his sexual demands.

One night, Rose was in her room with Albright when the house was raided by officers. Before escaping through a back window, Albright said she would be arrested soon enough and gave her money for the fine. When she later confessed she needed the affair to end, she said, "He drew out his revolver and told me to remember that he was a wicked man and that he would kill me."

Sending for the deputy United States marshal was futile; Albright couldn't be arrested without a warrant. Instead, Rose raced to the Knutsford Hotel, where Albright roomed, and immediately called for a policeman. When the officer arrived, he was told that Albright was a "desperate man." The initially hesitant officer found him to be cordial enough. But in passing Rose, Albright threatened her, she said. That night, the brothel was locked up tight when Albright tried to get in to see her.

The last time the two met, Albright was leaving on the Tuscarora train to Chicago. "He wanted me to go with him, and when I said I would not, [he] grew furious," she said. According to Rose, the officer drew his gun and, standing on the sidewalk, made threats to smash her face. Fortunately for the

Knutsford Hotel in downtown Salt Lake City. *Photograph used with permission from the Utah State Historical Society.*

prostitute, Albright was prevented from doing so by a nearby store owner, who witnessed the altercation. Albright vowed to get even when he returned. What Rose needed from the council was protection.

Finally

None of this was openly represented in court but permeated an unease in an otherwise easy case. During an investigation by his own police department, Albright was dismissed from the police force. Others were quickly fired. Just as quickly, some were reinstated. In the coming months, Rose would be arrested for keeping a brothel.

10

ANNIE PRINDLE REGRETS

PART ONE: SHE SHOT TO KILL

Vile and ingrate! Too late thou shalt repent the base injustice thou hast done my love. Yes, thou shalt know, spite of thy past distress, and all those ills, which thou so long hast mourn'd; Heav'n has no rage, like love to hatred turn'd, nor hell a fury, like a woman scorn'd.
—*William Congreve,* The Mourning Bride, *1697*

This is the story about a nurse named Annie Prindle, who, in a fit of jealousy or immaturity, was so smitten with a man that she desperately wanted to get her message across. Although the relationship appeared to be unrequited, and she was completely out of her depth, the young woman used a gun instead of her words.

Apparently, the May 5, 1891 *Salt Lake Herald-Republican* learned that thirty-five-year-old Sam Masterson, the owner of the Office Saloon on West Temple Street, located "across from the Grant Bros. stables," had paid a certain amount of attention to Annie until "she went out riding with another man." Put out, the saloon owner and Miss Prindle quarreled, and Masterson soon took up with another girl named Bertha Trim. "That," the paper informed, "was where he made a mistake."

Miss Trim, who roomed at the Columbia House on South Temple Street, and Mr. Masterson had made plans to attend a theater production. As star-crossed luck would have it, when Bertha arrived at the saloon's door to meet

C.E. Johnson, *Springtime Flowers. Photograph courtesy of the Special Collections, Merrill-Cazier Library, Utah State University.*

Sam, Annie, who was living in a boardinghouse room above the bar, caught a glimpse of her.

"[Annie] went into the [house] parlor and, after strumming on the organ a few minutes, went over to a bookcase and took out a loaded pistol," the *Salt Lake Herald-Republican* reported. Heading outside—she must have known the route the couple had taken—she easily intercepted them and began shouting that she wanted to talk to Masterson. Stunned, maybe Bertha and Sam began to turn away, or maybe Annie got just close enough, but when they were within ten feet of each other, Annie raised her pistol and, without warning, fired at Sam. The first bullet hit Masterson in his shoulder, and he collapsed in pain. Closing in on the couple, Annie fired again, this time hitting Sam's leg "below the groin." In all, four shots were fired. Only one missed its mark.

Hearing gunshots, Charles McCullen, the Office Saloon's bartender, raced out the back door and, seeing the fallen man, put his life on the line and grabbed Annie, who was still holding her gun. Although Annie threatened to shoot the bartender, too—who knew how many bullets were left in the chamber—McCullen restrained her until Officer Roberts, who was on patrol nearby on First South Street, rushed in, followed by two other officers. Overpowered and disarmed, the angry Miss Prindle was arrested.

Writhing with pain, Mr. Masterson was carried to a bedroom in the back of the saloon and examined by two doctors, including Dr. Frank Meacham.

"It was found that one [bullet] entered the back, near the shoulder blade, and glanced around to the front, inflicting a painful flesh wound," the *Salt Lake Herald-Republican* informed. Another struck his shoulder blade and the third, his leg. Although none were fatal, they were raw and throbbing.

When asked why she shot Sam, Annie blamed it on the "sheeny," a derogatory word aimed at Miss Trim. "And I want her arrested, too!" Annie said. Unrepentant—she wished she had killed them both—and self-assured, with only a glimmer of regret, the young woman spent the night in jail. Later, well dressed and calm while in court, Annie listened to witness testimonies, including that of the beleaguered Miss Trim. Annie looked distracted, maybe even amused and sometimes giggly.

Returning for her court trial on September 22, 1891, Annie pleaded guilty to assault with a deadly weapon. It was revealed that the victim, Sam Masterson, was fine. Annie received a sentence of six months. It was a light verdict, and the case was cut and dried.

Something about Sam Masterson

Sam Masterson was married. His wife, May, was a brothel keeper in a house of ill repute near the Rio Grande Western Depot. His luck with women had always been questionable. Having been told a week before that Annie was holding a grudge and a gun, he didn't pay attention.

Part Two: Annie Prindle Accuses

A Scandalous Pickle

Placed under the care and custody of United States marshal Elias H. Parsons, Annie Prindle was taken to the penitentiary, detained in the woman's ward and put into a cell that was reputedly occupied by prostitutes. Midway through her incarceration in early December, Annie accused Marshal Parsons of committing "diverse acts of inhumanity and oppression toward her." The marshal was indicted by the grand jury, and Annie, the territorial prisoner, found herself in an arresting court case portending issues of licentious mien, conspiracy, a women's reputation and prostitution—a scandalous pickle that, at this time, was anything but cut and dried.

The local papers went wild. On December 7, 1891, the *Deseret Evening News* lede shouted Marshall Parsons was accused of "soliciting the said Annie Prindle to lewdness with lascivious talk and conduct, and forcibly, indecently and against her will committed acts, laying hands upon her person, kissing and otherwise maltreating and subjecting her to great humiliation and indignity."

The Story, the Players

Within an hour after Marshal Parsons was served, he appeared before Commissioner H. Pratt to plead his case. An examination, conducted by the prosecuting attorney U.S. district attorney Charles S. Varian, was held behind closed doors. It must have taken some time, because along with an adjournment issued by the commissioner came a collective sigh.

In the waning days of suppressed Victorian sexuality, a large public crowd of men who were hungry for details that promised to be vivid and lurid hustled to Commissioner Pratt's courtroom, only to be turned away. Disgruntled, many milled around the hallways, waiting for an opportunity to become part of the audience. Others gathered outside to eavesdrop near the court's open windows.

The "high official and character assailed" case consumed numerous court days. The roster for the marshal's defense included attorneys Messrs. E.B. Critchlow, J.A. Rawlins and H.P. Henderson. Representing the prosecution against the marshal were the U.S. district attorney C.S. Varian and his assistant attorney, F.B. Stephens.

Elias Howard Parsons, the defendant, was a Union man and decorated Civil War veteran who was born in Massachusetts. After moving to Utah in the early 1870s, Parsons raised livestock, managed ranch properties and got involved in mining ventures. A Republican, he helped organize and became an ordained member of the First Presbyterian Church in Salt Lake City. While Utah was under a territorial government in 1889, Parsons became a most respected U.S. marshal.

Ironically, the December 8, 1891 *Ogden Daily Standard*, reporting on the marshal's indictment, discovered an additional and sweeping accusation:

> *The grand jury* [also] *filed an indictment against Parsons for maintaining a house for immoral purposes, and one against Brig*[ham] [Young] *Hampton for the same offense. Parsons is an alleged co-owner of a house*

in Plum Alley, which is allegedly rented to Chinese for gambling, opium
smoking and illicit commerce.

Tracking back six years to 1885, an adopted son of Brigham Young and an ardent member of Church of Jesus Christ of Latter-day Saints, Brigham Young Hampton was indeed engaged with a primarily LDS citizens' committee, dedicated to fleshing out those involved in lewd and lascivious conduct and, with the help of the city's police force, entrapping men seeking sexual pleasures. Taking the law into their own hands was an ill-advised and illegal endeavor. Mr. Hampton was apparently the only committee member who offered to take the hit in the district court. Sentenced to jail for one year, he wrote in his memoirs that he was treated kindly by his jailers. He never mentioned doing business with Mr. Parsons.[71]

What meaning proceeded with the indictment involving the implication of immorality in 1891 is up for grabs. But the condemnation that pitted a federal law enforcer's defense against a sexual complaint made by the young female prisoner serving a six-month sentence caused an upheaval in happenstance and a significant increase in newspaper readership.

"The sensational exposures in the Parsons investigation Friday were the talk of the city yesterday," the December 13, 1891 *Salt Lake Tribune* blared under the headline "All the Nastiness Brought Out by the Marshal's Own Witness." "[T]he universal opinion seemed to be that whether or not the marshal is guilty of the charges proffered against him by Annie Prindle and another prisoner, Maggie Forkner, the management of the penitentiary is such as to forever damn him as an official."

The lack of Marshal Parsons's testimony, which was taken behind closed doors, was challenging. Reporters doggedly foraged the trial case and recounted the nuts-and-bolts fundamentals garnered from witness gathering and testimonies to the detailed investigation of each slanderous incident.

Annie

Born in Minnesota, where, at one time, her parents had been farmers, Annie taught in a county school and cashiered in a large store in Minneapolis before she trained to become a nurse. When her mother, Jane Prindle, and her ailing father moved to West First North Street in Salt Lake City, where another of their daughters had been living, Annie eventually followed. The young woman's nursing skills and patient care services were not only in great demand but were also held in high esteem by patients, their families and the local Dr. Niles.

In this court case, representing the moral milieu of the 1890s, a person's reputation (or chastity) was considered of the utmost importance. When called to the witness stand, Mrs. Prindle said her daughter's reputation in Minnesota and Utah was in good standing. Anna's sister agreed. When the nurse was incarcerated, whatever they may have felt or said, both mother and sister continued to visit Annie.

Admittedly, Annie attempted to shoot Sam Masterson, she said, in a bout of jealousy—because Masterson "went with other girls"—but she had never been criminally intimate with the man. He had been her friend. At the time, she said she'd been drinking but "not with Masterson or other men; it was only while in jail that she discovered he might have been married." Penning a letter to him from her cell proved futile. He never responded to her nor appeared in court.

The Complaint: A Sequence of Uninvited Advances

September 22: Annie was taken to the penitentiary and, as recorded in the December 14, 1891 *Deseret Evening News*, was escorted into Marshal E.H. Parsons's private office, where she was introduced by the warden, Mr. Vandercook. After the warden left, Annie remained with Parsons for nearly two hours.

The plaintiff held that Marshal Parsons told her he was sorry she had been taken to the reformatory. He promised to do what he could to make her confinement pleasant, and since he had nearby relatives, he proposed she might be able to stay with them.

"He wanted to be a friend to me after my term had expired and more than a friend to me during my imprisonment," Annie said under oath. Taking liberties, he kissed and embraced her. "I pushed him away."

Later that night, the marshal took Annie to his relatives, the Giesys' (also written up as Geysey or Giesey), home, where she was welcomed. The next day, the marshal returned her to the penitentiary.

September 27: The following Sunday, the marshal kissed and embraced Annie and then, Annie testified in a quiet, straightforward manner, "acted rudely, [said] he wanted to get at me as soon as possible." This would later be interpreted by Parsons's defense team as a calculated lie. Annie said the marshal knew when the Giesys were away from home "and that he intended to come out on such an occasion and have me stay with him. I told him not to do it, or there would sure be trouble."

October 17: A baffling incident occurred in the Giesys' kitchen. It was a full house. Many extended family members, including Mr. Parsons's wife, had congregated there. Some talked in the sitting room, while others were in the cellar looking for canned goods: fruit, peppers, bottled pickles. Kids were running around. Amid all of this, the marshal and Annie were in the kitchen, where he, regretting there were people in the house, once again took liberties. He "laid hold of her limbs," the *Deseret News* reported. "She resisted and 'kicked' him from the very first."

On or about October 22: Annie was brought into Marshal Parsons's private office. Several people were coming in and out for one thing or another. "When there was no one, [the marshal] took me on his knee and held me to him and again acted rudely," Annie said. "Mr. Giesy came in, and the marshal sent him on an errand. I went across the room and sat on the lounge. [The marshal then] came up to me, exposed himself, disarranged my clothing and made grossly indecent proposals." Once outside the marshal's office, the young woman waited for Mr. Giesy to take her back to the penitentiary.

Annie finally disclosed the marshal's misdeeds to Warden Vandercook. He may have been sympathetic, but he had been given a "positive order" by the marshal to return her to the Giesys' home or to her cell. She chose to be locked up. The warden did suggest she stay at his home, and it's probable she may have done this for about a week.

November 10: In what was most likely the last incident at the penitentiary, Annie felt sickly. Dr. Smith, who arrived with the marshal, ordered her to be confined to her bed for a week.

"[The marshal] remained in my cell until the doctor went out," Annie said. "Then he put his hands under my bed clothes, kissed me and said he was sorry to see me sick."

The U.S. marshal's alleged misconduct with Annie, who affirmed its validity, "affected her mentally" and reinforced fears that she was unable to defend herself and was uncontrollably at the whim of Marshal Parsons. Telling her family nothing about the abuse, Annie confided in female inmates, including the alleged prostitute Maggie Forkner.

The Matter of Chastity Mattering

According to the December 26, 1891 *Deseret Weekly*, Parsons's defense attorney Mr. Henderson addressed the allegations against the marshal. "He said a charge had been made against a high officer of this territory, which involved not only his morality, his standing as a man, but which affected his standing as an officer, and if it were true, it stamped him as one absolutely without honor." That statement alone ignited an urgent rush to find witnesses for the defense.

Culling from a list of potential eyewitnesses, the *Deseret Evening News* reported that Parsons's defense team called Clarence Wolfington to the stand. Mr. Wolfington, who was known to work as an extra bartender, had once taken over Masterson's place behind the bar for a week while the man recovered from a sprained wrist. When asked about Miss Prindle, Wolfington said he knew a "woman named Annie who used to be around the place when I was there." When Mr. Henderson questioned Annie's "general reputation for chastity and morality," the temporary barkeep replied it was "bad." When cross-examined by the prosecutor Mr. Varian, the bartender professed, "I don't wish to convey the impression that she was, at the time, what could be called a public prostitute," he said before settling on the fact that Annie was a "private prostitute."

Just how much the extra bartender could have known about Annie, having filled in at the bar for only one week, gives one pause. Explaining his reliance on what he picked up from an assortment of the saloon's regular drinkers, Wolfington said they made vulgar and suggestive jokes, "talked about Annie's ongoing visits to the saloon, and going down to the wine room of the saloon a good many times, talking to men and drinking whiskey with them."

Although Masterson commented that Annie was a "square" woman, Wolfington was not convinced of her reputation or his interest in the woman. "She claimed to be taking typewriting lessons," Wolfington said, "and yet occupied a great part of her time in the wine room of the saloon drinking. I thought it rather peculiar that a woman who was taking typewriting lessons should be drinking whiskey."

Mr. Wolfington mentioned a Mr. Scheil (or Schell), whom he said knew her better and concluded "it would be impossible to pull [Annie] much lower than she was at that time, if you ask me."

The extra bartender then told defense attorney Henderson that he had been arrested in Leadville, Colorado, for murder. He said the incident had to do with someone being rude to his wife and happened before Ms. Prindle's case came up. "Tried and acquitted by the jury," he also admitted to being charged with assault with a deadly weapon while in Utah and "held to answer before a grand jury." That case, he said, "was dismissed."

On December 26, 1891, the *Deseret Weekly* reported that Mr. Scheil was interrogated by defense attorney Mr. Rawlins.

A brickmaker from East Bountiful who often patronized Masterson's tavern, Mr. Scheil first met Ms. Prindle in October 1890. He was aware of Mr. Masterson's private room and had seen Annie entering the wine room nearly every day for some five months, sometimes noticing her in the lounge in the mornings and coming out of Masterson's private room at night. He surmised Annie may have also been a chambermaid for Mrs. Vincent, who had rooms above the saloon. According to the paper, "This line of evidence was objected to by the prosecutor and sustained by the commissioner, maintaining he did not think counsel could show the woman's reputation by a specific act. It must be by general acts."

Mrs. Mattie Vincent rented furnished rooms on West Temple above Masterson's saloon. There was no indication that she ran rooms for prostitutes. In her testimony, she told the prosecuting assistant attorney Mr. Stephens that she met Ms. Prindle while the nurse was caring for her ailing sister. She considered the woman's reputation good, and for nearly a year, while she was continuing her work as a nurse, Annie resided in Mrs. Vincent's boardinghouse.

The newspaper noted that Mrs. Vincent "was not aware that Annie Prindle was in a [steady] habit of going down to Masterson's saloon but had the occasion to speak to the young woman about Masterson's [reputation] prior to the shooting and advised her 'not to keep company' with him." (Ironically, Mrs. Vincent was the first to question Annie's violent intentions when she was brought to her room for a change of clothes before being taken to jail.)

And yes, Mrs. Vincent said she had seen Ms. Prindle in the saloon but certainly "not more than a dozen times." At this point, the commissioner intervened, saying the counsel "was launching a little too much into detail."

Another witness was James A. Williams, an attorney and transplant from Kentucky who was working in Salt Lake City. He was introduced to Annie while she was nursing his friend Attorney Kooms during the last stages of an illness that would take his life. Mr. Williams maintained Annie's conduct was "quite ladylike in any way that could be desired."

After escorting his friend's casket to his family and attending his funeral in the East, Williams returned to Salt Lake City. Picking up Williams's testimony, the December 14 *Deseret Evening News* related the man "denied receiving letters from Miss Prindle inviting him to meet her and declared that he had never been on anything more than the terms of an ordinary acquaintance." Furthermore, the attorney wanted it "clearly understood that he was not the Mr. Williams said to have called upon Annie during her stay at the Giesys' residence."

In her defense, Annie expressed that two people, a bartender named Mr. Daniels and Mr. Williams, a "mining man" and "sporting guy" accompanied by a woman friend, did call on her. They were loud and brash men, and the visitation took place in the daytime. Neither man bore gifts of cigars or cigarettes, although one extinguished his cigarette at Mrs. Giesy's stern admonition. Mr. Daniel suggested starting a petition "to obtain her pardon." But Annie never asked for a pardon.

Responding to a witness's remark about her habit of smoking cigars, Annie also explained she smoked as a preventive measure to avoid being compromised when treating a patient with a contagious disease. Otherwise, she rarely partook. She said it was never a habit.

When penitentiary guard E.R. Field was called by the prosecution, he stated he knew Annie as a prisoner and "never had inappropriate contact with her and never saw anything wrong on her part there," according to the December 26 *Deseret Weekly*. The report added, "The witness gave his evidence on this point most emphatically."

There was a female prisoner named only as "Hanks," who, according to Maggie Forkner, "told the warden that [Annie] had been criminally intimate with the guards." There was an allegation of a duplicate key made that opened women's cells, allowing easy access for free-range male convicts "picnicking" in the corridors to peer into and enter female cells. Guards were questioned. These contentions and others provoked both the defense and prosecution teams into a verbal scrimmage before the assertions fizzled.

Other witnesses came forward. Miss Prindle's respectable nursing skills were again highlighted. Few outside the penitentiary knew about her calamity with the tavern owner, and hardly anyone else—other than the extra bartender, hearsay from saloon frequenters, perhaps even Annie's traumatized mother and the marshal's defense team (intending to grind her down)—declared Annie a fallen woman.

Reprisal, Conspiracy, Dogged Reputation and Energetic Orations

Focusing on the extra bartender Wolfington's sworn testimony, prosecuting attorney Varian made short shrift of the man's declaration. "They [the defense] brought a man who was tried for murder in Colorado [and] who spent a month awaiting trial there. They brought him here, but for what?" the prosecutor asked. "Not that he knew [Annie's] reputation, but people [who] said she was guilty of having intercourse with Masterson and when [the extra bartender] was pinned down, [it] simply amounted to what he heard said by a man named L., whom nobody heard of before or since."

Picked up by the December 17 *Salt Lake Tribune* was the defense team's claim of "a great conspiracy." If such treachery existed, its roots certainly showed up in the remarks circulated by female prisoners, such as Essie Banks's last-minute testimony, which was taken to task during prosecutor Varian's four-hour argument. "There was that 'estimable' Essie Banks, upon her cot in her cell adjoining that of Annie Prindle and Miss Forkner," Mr. Varian said. He summed up Banks's story and exposed the woman's perversion with her description of an inside guard, Mr. Stark.

Banks maintained Stark entered Annie's cell before going down to the grand jury. "They have a conversation," Varian recounted:

> [Essie] *hears Mr. Stark say to say to them, "Now, what are you going to do before the grand jury?"* I [the prosecutor] *don't give the exact language, but this is the substance of it: "Stick together, and we will clinch the old S.O.B." That is the way Essie says they described the marshal, adding that Annie said, "I will swear to do anything to get this S.O.B." Now then, it was known to the marshal that at the time the witness was on the stand,* [her statement was] *a blushing perjury. There is no escaping from it. He* [the marshal] *himself had taken Stark in his buggy and took him downtown. He knew Stark never could have been back in that cell that morning.*

With Essie Banks exposed as being untruthful, the December 26 *Deseret Weekly* made clear that prosecutor Mr. Varian had more to say:

> *They* [the defense] *were permitted to show, to a certain extent, specific acts* [told] *by this woman* [Banks], *whom they brought here—this keystone to this alleged conspiracy—and the alleged acts with the guard. Every latitude was given to them. Now, after six or seven witnesses* [called

on] *to meet the question of* [Annie's] *general reputation had been presented, they would seek to interject this unknown,* [untruthful] *witness at the end of the case.*

Speaking to the character of Prindle, "upon which the defense mounted its attack," Mr. Varian argued, "they had taken the mantle of Essie Banks, and they brought it down here and attempted to fit it upon Annie Prindle and it did not fit." Busting the great conspiracy myth as hollow, the prosecutor built up momentum and, in a moment of fiery speech, shouted:

> *You stand up here now and attack this woman's* [Prindle's] *reputation in this community, and we throw down the bars to you.... Throw your deputy marshals into the houses of prostitution and bring up your witnesses if you like. Where are the women who keep houses of prostitution who know her? Bring them in if you can....But we propose to confine you to the rules and laws of evidence.*

"When Mr. Varian had exhausted himself," the paper reported, "[Parsons's defense attorney] Mr. Rawlins went to the wickets. He had been worked up to a high pitch of excitement by the words of the [prosecuting] attorney, and thus opened fire upon the adversary, beginning with Annie and her gun":

> *We propose to show that this woman* [Prindle] *entered by the back door* [of the saloon] *and remained there overnight with the saloonkeeper. We propose to show her habits. We propose to show how bad she had fallen, her state of degradation...her reputation in that den of vice.*

Mr. Rawlins would have continued in this manner had the commissioner not struck his remarks, repeating his ruling that "counsel may show the general reputation, but they cannot show specific acts to affect that general reputation."

Addressing the unrelenting attacks on Annie Prindle by Parsons's defense team and their efforts to destroy Annie's already fragile reputation, Mr. Varian said their motives had gone too far, to which Mr. Rawlins refuted, bellowing that she:

> *is not helpless at all. She is brought here as a sword to attack the life and character of the defendant. She is brought here and permitted to say, in various forms, that...indecent proposals were made to her such as no man*

*would make unless a brute in human form, and we "have to" meet this.
We have a right to test her reputation, I say, even during the time she was a
prisoner of the petitionary.*

His remarks were overruled.

No Doubts?

The attorneys' battlefield was aflame with ambiguous contention and sprinkled with outrageous conjectures and frustrating slap-downs by the commissioner. "There was an insinuation [by defense attorney] Mr. Rawlings to the effect that the witness [Annie] used to sit in her cell in an indecent posture and smoke cigarettes," the December 14 *Deseret Evening News* shared. "This elicited an indignant look from the witness and a warm retort from the prosecuting attorney" was supported by the commissioner who, not amused, reiterated rule of law.

And what of the evidence? In the December 17 *Salt Lake Tribune*, "Defense Attorney Critchlow determined that Maggie Forkner—who also accused the marshal of impropriety and likely in pursuit of a pardon—was a harlot and a liar.…This 'abandoned woman, the product of spews, had engaged in attempt to besmirch the character of an official here and says that her virtue has been outraged. It was a sorry spectacle, enough to make gods and devils laugh.'"

For Miss Prindle, who was already halfway through her prison sentence, defense attorney Mr. Critchlow, entered the oratorial arena, protesting that "he would not hang a yellow dog upon the word of such a creature."

Accusations of blackmail and downright perjury on the part of the women prisoners were slanderous enough but still provoked the defense team's contention that they were "not allowed to prove that [Annie] was unchaste by showing she lived in a brothel and frequented saloons."

Changing direction, prosecutor Varian questioned why "the marshal's brother-in-law, his guard, his dependent, Mr. Giesy," was not called upon to testify. Left hanging, he spoke to the "absence of testimony, shown to be within reach, and which of necessity [might] throw light one way or the other upon the question [as] a legitimate subject of argument and interference."

Point by point, prosecuting attorney Varian honed his argument and magnified each issue of incongruency proffered by a defense team that continued to chisel away at Annie Prindle's reputation.

The trial ran until the end of the eighth day. In closing, when the defense counsels represented their case, Marshal Parsons was in court. But when Mr. Varian "opened the floodgates of his oratory," the marshal retired to Pratt's office, where he paced back and forth until his nerves got the better of him. He then returned to the courtroom and sat in a chair with his back to the proceedings.

The Wrap-Up

In a grouping of the aforementioned local newspaper accounts, the commissioner (and judge) Mr. Pratt said he was impressed by Annie, who gave her testimony at the stand, "as being a fair, candid witness and one disposed to tell the truth. Another strong impression was how she related the events at the Giesy home. These facts are strong points in the prosecution." The "weak point" that didn't impress the commissioner, he revealed, "included the public manner in which she alleged these attacks were committed. Three attacks of this nature committed upon her before she says anything about it."

Addressing the alleged shameful and violent incident at the Giesys' home, the commissioner was most impressed by the testimony of Mrs. R.A. Giesy. "She heard the marshal coming while he was yet on the road," he said. "Then she returned to the sitting room. She had him in view from the time he entered the kitchen, practically, until he went into the cellar, where his wife was. She testified positively that it would be impossible for the marshal to have touched Annie Prindle."

Annie Prindle was, "in the commissioner's opinion, unworthy of belief in one instance, [and thus] her whole testimony should be considered as false."

That was it.

Marshal E. Parsons was discharged. Exonerated, he "passed into the street to proclaim his 'innocence' to all who cared to listen," reported the *Salt Lake Tribune.*

And then the presses went silent.

Annie Prindle and her case remain an enigma. After battling a whirlwind of hearsay and rumor, the prosecution determined there was no ample amount of evidence to affirm that Annie was a prostitute, patroness of many saloons, conspirator or easy woman displaying herself behind bars. Why then, after all was laid bare, did nothing not hold weight or bear on the marshal's credibility?

Facing off against a well-recognized and highly regarded marshal, was it possible that the restrictive mores of ethics and morals—the notion of a young, single woman reportedly having had a sexual relationship—was enough to impugn Annie's reputation?

The following year, in 1892, E.H. Parsons retired from his post. Around 1898, according to archives at Brigham Young University's Harold B. Library, Parsons was called "to assist in the U.S. Armed Forces" during the Spanish-American War and the Philippine Insurrection.[72] The Parsons family later moved to California.

Annie Prindle hopefully finished her prison term unharmed and was released.

11

RADISHES, ONIONS AND SEX

THE TRIAL OF OLD BEN

This is the court case and winding tale of Gee Ben, a Chinese man who wanted a young girl; two underaged girls "wanting a dime's worth of radishes and onions"; a married man accused of rape who wanted excuses; a city detective; a couple of local newspaper reporters; a zealous audience, including a sobbing young wife; and a shadowy woman or two who goaded the girls to trade sex for money.[73]

PART ONE: CARNAL KNOWLEDGE, SEPTEMBER 30, 1903, 2:53 P.M.

Warrants of Arrests and Subpoenas

The crime of felony, as follows, to-wit: The said Old [Gee] Ben did on the 9th day of June, A.D. 1903 at Ogden City, in the County of Weber and State of Utah, then and there have carnal knowledge of the body of Lizzie Peterson, she being a female over the age of thirteen years and under the age of eighteen years and not the wife of said Old Ben, and he did then and there have sexual intercourse with and carnally know and abuse said Lizzie Peterson.
—State of Utah v. Warrant of Arrest, *second district court, Weber County, case no. 347, filed October 10, 1903.*

In Court: Judge J.A. Howell of the Municipal Court of Ogden City presided. County attorney F.T. Hulaniski Esq. appeared as counsel for the prosecution; Messrs. Henderson and MacMillian appeared for the defendant. The victim, Lizzie Peterson, was the prosecutrix and chief witness (along with her ally Mary Ellen Jenkins) in what was considered a most sordid case.

Where to Begin

On June 6, 1903, Lizzie Peterson, fifteen, and her friend Mary Ellen Jenkins, sixteen, were loitering by the Eccles Mill and Lumber Yard in Ogden when they caught the sight of a Mr. and Mrs. Barnard and ran over to ask if they could sleep at their place. "We didn't have any bed," Lizzie explained to the court, "and she says, yes; [that] as long as she had a shelter, we could have one, too." Mr. Barnard was heading home with a "bucket of beer, and Mrs. Barnard told him to light a fire." Lizzie recalled, "And [we] would go to the store for sugar or butter or something."

The girls also spoke of a "Mrs. Lindsay," who apparently lived in the same house that Mary Ellen's Aunt Kate had been living in on Twenty-Eighth Street. Walking toward it, they discovered it was the wrong house and turned around. At the Barnards' house, Mrs. Barnard told her husband to begin making dinner while they went to "Ben's to get radishes and onions."

The Chinese gardener Gee Ben had his own house and garden in a back alley on Twenty-Ninth Street between Adams and Jefferson Streets. With basket in hand, Mrs. Barnard led the two girls toward the brickyard, and from there, Lizzie said they "waded through water and mud clear up to our knees and over a fence and every other thing, and when we got over there, Mrs. Lindsay said she wanted some radishes and onions." (Oddly, no one questions the authenticity of a Mrs. Lindsay when the teenagers were talking about Mrs. Barnard.)

The girls sat on a vegetable box, waiting for Mr. Gee Ben to put the produce in the basket. "Mrs. Lindsay" told Lizzie that Gee Ben would give $5.00 for a young girl. "She says, 'I was over here a while ago, and he gave me $2.50, but if he could get a young girl, he will give her $5.00,'" Lizzie told the judge.

Gee Ben first asked Mary if she would go with him. Mary was not up for it, which infuriated Mrs. Lindsay enough to shout, "You go on—go on, you damn fool! That's five dollars!"

When Mary was called on by the prosecution, she added, "Then she winked at the Chinaman, [saying] 'Ain't [Lizzie] a good-looking girl?' And the Chinaman says, 'A fine-looking girl.'"

"Mrs. Lindsay said I was her daughter," Lizzie acknowledged, but when Gee Ben offered her five dollars to go with him, she, too, said no. And Mrs. Lindsay was again frustrated.

> *"Go on," she says, and I says, "I don't want to," and she says, "Go on—go on," and I don't know what to do. We were sitting on some tomato boxes. He went into the house and brought out a little bowl, or a glass, I don't know which, about two-thirds full of whiskey and handed it to Mary. Mary handed it to me. I handed to Mrs. Barnard. She drank it up and says, "Hurry up, now, and come on," and I says, "I don't want to," and Mrs. Lindsay says, "Go on, that's five dollars, you need it!" And I sat there [for] a minute, and I didn't know what to do. So, I went.*

Gee Ben guided Lizzie over a ditch to the other side of his house, where, outside his home, the two had sexual intercourse. Ten minutes later, Lizzie returned with five dollars in silver. "Five dollars, and we didn't go through the brickyard. We went around on Jefferson [Street]," she said. "'Let's go now,' Mrs. Lindsay said."

During the court proceedings, Lizzie spoke of the second time she and Mary met with Gee Ben. It was June 8, around 8:00 p.m., and they may have gone there out of curiosity.

"We went over there to get some radishes and onions," Lizzie told the court. "We told him we wanted a dime's worth, and he asked me again, and I told him I didn't want to. 'Oh, come on,' he says." The first time another Chinese gentleman visited Gee Ben's home, Old Ben and Lizzie obliged their assignation taken outside the house. This time, the visitor was gone. The two went into the house.

According to Lizzie, Gee Ben offered $2.50 if Lizzie went with him and $5.00 the next time. "We done the same as we had done the first time," she said. Mary heard the gardener say he would give Lizzie $2.00 and that Lizzie wouldn't do it for $2.00. "'Yes, $2.00,' he says. 'That's enough this time.' 'No, I won't,' she says. 'Well,' he says, 'I'll give you $2.50 then.'"

Mary watched as they went through one door and another into a small bedroom. "They went in there, and I went and peeked in the corner where there was a crack about this wide [*showing the width of her hand*], and Lizzie lay crossways on the bed." Lizzie's clothes were up. The man was on top of her.

While they may have discussed not telling Mrs. Lindsay about Lizzie's tryst with Gee Ben, Lizzie did just that, and the woman was pleased and said it was good.

Street Walking Leads to Arrest

It's not uncommon that dates and times are often ephemeral, misrepresented, discredited or downright difficult to remember. Lizzie tended to count backward from a significant and personal event, dates that were immediately backed up by Mary. As a result, it was determined the two girls had been on the streets for over a year or two years and had spent most of the summer, since May, "running together." But it was hard to say. On an aunt's recommendation, Mary, who had been living in California, was in Utah to marry a man, who, the very next morning, threatened to kill her. He was arrested and fined, and on May 4, Mary stayed with relatives in Ogden.

Lizzie, whose mother and stepfather resided in Ogden, confessed to rarely being with them at their home, choosing instead to run the streets or stay at a friend's house behind the pickle factory on Wall Street. Mary reaffirmed the defendant's account that they were meeting boys and men.

Prior to visiting the Chinese gardener—or a day earlier or after, blurring mindful timelines—the girls were walking between Twenty-Fourth and Twenty-Fifth Streets and met with four fellows, including one named Rockefeller. After the girls invited the men to the Barnards' home, the six played cards and listened to music and one of the boys, who played the mouth organ. They may have gotten rowdy. A neighbor called the police, saying they were disturbing the peace.

On June 9, 1903, the *Ogden Daily Standard* reported that "the girls have been under surveillance of the officers for some time and were arrested because they have continuously walked the streets and been found where suspicion of the most immoral conduct was aroused." Given that their ages were taken to be under fourteen years, they had a hearing before Judge Howell; they were sent to the district court and deemed candidates for the state industrial school.[74]

"We were arrested on the 9th of June down on Lincoln and 24th Streets for running on the streets, I guess," Lizzie elaborated to the court on the morning of September 30.

> *They took us over here* [to the district court], *and* [we were] *taken to the city jail. We was* [sic] *over to the county a while, and they made out some papers, and* [we were taken] *to the reform school. We were out there*

for five days, and after that, we came into town and had a trial here and we went over to the county jail and had a trial. They let me go, and they took Mary to the Crittenton Home. I was working. I got some money. Ma wanted it, and I thought I wanted it, so I kept it and ran away and went down to [my friends'] *the Brooks' house behind the pickle factory.*

Three days later, City Detective J.F. Pender, who often cautioned the girls "to be good," pinpointed Lizzie's location and found her. The young girl spent some two days in jail before eventually being taken to the Crittenton Home on July 1, 1903.

Redemption?

Incorporated in 1897 in Ogden and merged with the existing Home of the Friendless, the Florence Crittenton Mission (called the Crittenton Home) offers its services in over sixty other American cities and in four "foreign countries." Its mission is to "Save girls who err…who are led astray…and others to escape from the pitfalls and evil influences of great cities, to rescue the perishing and lift up the fallen."

Lizzie was mum about the incident with the Chinese man until she wound up at the Crittenton Home. After giving her testimony, the September 22, 1903 *Ogden Daily Standard* reported that she "confessed that her indiscretion had led to her ruin and that she was in a delicate condition," although there was no mention of the indiscretion or what it meant—or that it was even taken up in court. Lizzie and Mary "admitted they had been street walkers for the past two years."

"Mary told up to the home that we went there," Lizzie told the court. "[After] a while, I told Mrs. Adams [possibly a counselor], and two or three weeks later, she phoned down and told Mr. Pender about it."

Detective Pender often warned the girls to get off the street. On one occasion, after seeing them by the Salvation Army Hall with two men, he told the girls to run home, or they'd be taken to jail or sent to the reform school.

It was after 9:00 p.m., and "we were just going to the Salvation Army Hall, or they were on their way out," Mary said. "Lizzie was talking with the men who pointed a twenty-dollar [bill] right in our face." Mary believed they wanted to take the girls out for dinner, but "Mr. Pender says, 'Now, I want you to go home as fast as you can.' I ran across the street and went home." She didn't know what Lizzie did.

Gee Ben, Little Woman, Big Belly

As for Gee Ben, Mr. Pender said "the defendant, stated in the presence of the chief of police and [me that he] had given the girl here five dollars; for that, Mrs. Lindsay had told him that she was her daughter and had brought the girl up there but didn't say what it was for." Apparently, Gee Ben "spoke plain enough to be understood at that time."

While under arrest at the police station, the Chinese gardener glimpsed Mrs. Lindsay and, speaking to Mr. Pender, said, "Jim, little woman, big belly, son-a-ka-bitch; [said] that was her girl; give her $5." Admitting his guilt at the time, Gee Ben was bound over for trial; his bail was set at $1,000.

When the counsel for the defense asked if it was the first time Lizzie had anything to do with a man or a boy, the prosecuting attorney objected, saying that question was "incompetent, irrelevant and immaterial." The defense claimed it lent "to the credibility of her testimony and her truthfulness." He then asked if, on May 30, Lizzie had a connection with a man called Rockefeller. The prosecuting attorney again objected and moved to strike out the question. None of which, it seems, would be forgotten.

Part Two: Smoke Screens

One in the Same

On July 5, 1902, Mary A. Lindsay married Clifford H. Barnard. The marriage application was signed by Mary A. Darwin. Unable to write his name, Clifford made an X, and next to it, Mary penned his signature. Each one swore neither was married. According to the July 8 *Daily Standard*, by marrying a second husband, Darwin-Lindsay-Barnard had "thereby willfully and feloniously committed the crime of polygamy, on which charge a warrant has been issued for her arrest."

Five months earlier, Mary's first husband, Dan Lindsay, had left the City of Ogden and his wife to work on a power plant in American Falls, Idaho, along the edge of the Snake River. Upon his return, Mr. Lindsay discovered that another person had taken his place in "his wife's affections." Immediately filing a complaint with Justice Parker J. Hall, a warrant was issued for the arrest of Mary, a woman who was already well known in police court cases for "drunkenness and frequenting wine rooms." Was she truly a polygamist?

In 1881, Dan had been living in Nephi, Utah, when he brought Mary Darwin over from London. After living together as husband and wife for fifteen years, they decided to move to Ogden. According to the October 22, 1903 *Daily Standard*, however, the couple had never married, although one witness, a neighbor, who had known them for years, disagreed.

Defending herself, Mrs. Lindsay/Barnard asserted she and Dan were not married and never had been. "No," she said to the witness, "you or no one else saw me married; not to Dan Lindsay, anyhow." She was acquitted and discharged.

But her problems continued to mount, and one must wonder: Was the consistent name game used as a distraction, a ploy to confuse? Was she nefarious, a trafficker of young girls, a procuress of whomever was at hand? Or was she all the aforementioned? The papers would call it "a revolting case."

Mrs. Barnard's Debacle

The crime of felony, as follows, to-wit: The said Mary Barnard did on the 9th day of June 1903…then and there feloniously aid, counsel, encourage, abet, assist and advise a certain Chinaman called Old Ben, he being a male over eighteen years old, to have sexual intercourse with and to carnally know and abuse Lizzie Peterson, she being a female over thirteen years of age.
—State of Utah v. Warrant of Arrest, *second district court, Weber County, case no. 346, filed October 10, 1903*

September 30, 1903, 4:00 p.m.: Unable to afford counsel, Mrs. Barnard asked the court to appoint one to her. But she was told the court has no authority to do so. When the prosecution called Lizzie to the stand, she said the first time she had seen Mrs. Barnard occurred when she was arrested. She quickly amended the date of this encounter to June 6, when she and Mary had been looking for a place to spend the night. Going over her testimony, she summarized being at Gee Ben's house, the route they took and Mrs. Barnard's insistence that she go with the gardener, which, despite protests, she did for five dollars.

Mary was then asked by the prosecution if any of Lizzie's money went to Mrs. Barnard. Although Mrs. Barnard asked for no money, she apparently told the girls they had "no butter or coal" at the house. And according to Mary, the following morning, about $2.50 of Lizzie's ill-gained money was "expended" on behalf of Mrs. Barnard. Her purchases included cheese, butter, eggs, salmon, lemon cake and "two buckets of beer and whiskey" that Mr. Bernard had gone downtown to get.

The court asked Mrs. Barnard if she had a question for Mary, and she did: "Where did that whiskey come in at?" she asked. Mary repeated: "Mr. Bernard went downtown after it."

At this, Mrs. Bernard charged, "Now you know that you are lying?"

The court admonished, "Hold on, now, Mrs. Barnard. Just ask her questions. Don't contradict her."

"When did he go?" the defendant Barnard asked.

"He went down that evening," Mary replied.

"He did not," the defendant demanded. Again, the court insisted she not contradict the witness and instead "just ask the question." This was difficult for Mrs. Barnard to accomplish since she was steadfast and vocal in her defense.

"Where did you get the radishes and onions that you brought to the house?" she asked.

"We got them of [*sic*] you, Mrs. Barnard," Mary said.

"No. You had them when you came to my house."

"No, we didn't," Mary answered.

The court tried to help Mrs. Barnard formalize her style of questioning, which was not going well, as it was mired by her impregnable nature and lack of legal conduct.

Mrs. Barnard denied eating the food the girls purchased. "Whatever you got, you got for yourselves. You didn't get anything for us."

The court, intervening, asked Mary, "Is that so?"

"No, sir," she replied.

Mrs. Barnard probed, negated, refuted and defended herself in every case in point, and each time, she was reproached by the court. "I don't know that I want to ask her anymore [questions]," she said.

Deciding she had had it, Mrs. Barnard gave what amounted to be her own testimony to the court, although it wasn't required during this preliminary examination.

> *I want to say, I didn't take the girls there. The girls had been there before they came to my house; that's why they told me; I don't know only what they said. I wasn't with them, but when I went over there for these radishes and onions, I said I was going for some, and they asked if they could go with me, and of course, I simply said yes, and they went over there with me. But*

as far as I am concerned, there's nothing when I saw that they—not that I saw. I didn't see anything done and didn't hear of anything.

Warned by the court that her testimony may be used against her in the case trial held in the district court or may even be stricken out, Mrs. Barnard was adamant until, finally, she was truly exhausted and had nothing more to say.

The prosecuting attorney did, however. "I ask that she be bound over and the same bond be fixed. This is a more heinous offense than the other one, if anything." The court ordered the sum of $1,000 for her release.

PART THREE: 1-2-3 CRIMINALS

September 30: Gee Ben and Mrs. Barnard were bound over to the district court. Gee Ben, whose lawyer was Mr. Henderson, might not have understood the workings of the court, its "American idea of justice, its language, syntax and innuendos." The court entered a plea of not guilty. On October 21, Mrs. Barnard realized her fate.

Then there was the bombshell: the elusive John V. Rockefeller, who was accused of assaulting Lizzie in a cemetery or park on May 30. He didn't believe he was guilty of anything.

Rockefeller's Folly

Calling the crime an "unsavory rape case," the September 30, 1903 *Ogden Daily Standard* reported that Rockefeller's alleged victim, Lizzie, spoke of the assault and said she "had made no resistance but that Rockefeller had offered her money afterwards but did not make [good] his promise." Lizzie broke into tears during her testimony, and the paper noted it was the more often the prosecutrix who "had the appearance of brazen indifference."

When the defense attorney W.L. McGinnis assembled the testimony of five Rockefeller family members, the defendant's wife, holding her newborn, cried often but turned out to be a credible witness for her husband. The others, including his brother Jesse, testified Rockefeller was with them during the afternoon of the assault, and furthermore, there would not have been enough time for Rockefeller to go the distance necessary to do such a despicable deed. John V. Rockefeller pleaded not guilty to the charge. Setting his trial date for October 21, Judge Howell took the case under advisement.

The Procuress Is Tried

In the district court before Judge Henry H. Rolapp, Mary Lindsay-Bernard went on trial before a jury. J.D. Skeen represented the defendant, and District Attorney Halverson represented the state. When Bernard's case was called, Skeen moved the court to have the witnesses on both sides and the public escorted from the room. The court acquiesced to one, but as the October 20 *Ogden Daily Standard* reported, "As far as excluding the public, if there was anyone that wanted to come into the court room and listen to a dirty story, [the court agreed] to let them do so."

Most inquisitive spectators did leave the courtroom, save for Clifford Barnard and Lindsay/Barnard's former "husband," Dan Lindsay.

During the trial, Lizzie told her story with clarity, revealing the criminal trickery of Barnard/Lindsay and Lizzie's downfall and ruination by Gee Ben. She identified Rockefeller, occasionally putting her head in her hands and weeping, possibly for not realizing the shame and disgrace of her undoing. The jurors were captivated, bewildered and, ofttimes, puzzled.

Within three minutes the following day, Mrs. Mary A. Barnard was found guilty of acting as a procuress for Gee Ben. "The verdict was received with some show of surprise by Clifford Barnard and Dan Lindsay," reported the October 21 *Ogden Daily Standard*. "They both shook her hands very fervently and spoke cheering words to her, but the result did not seem to bother her at all. And with her indifferent air, she walked beside a deputy sheriff to her cell in the county jail." In a conflicting message, it seems Mrs. Barnard was indeed agitated and, while waiting in her cell for her court date, could barely eat.

Can't Take His Eyes Off of Her

During the trial, Rockefeller sat near his attorneys W.L. McGinnis and Chas. Stout. The October 21 *Ogden Daily Standard* noted that he "very often entered into deep conversation with them." He also kept his gaze on Lizzie and, "once or twice, smiled as some of the disgusting testimony was given."

Hearing evidence from his family that afternoon, the state listened to three more witnesses, including the accused. Rockefeller insisted he had never been with the "complaining witness," who, he believed, was fallacious in her account. Further, he had numbers of family members testifying on his behalf.

"The man who is alleged to have criminally assaulted Lizzie Peterson," blared the October 23 *Ogden Daily Standard*, following the case to its conclusion. "When the word *guilty* fell from the clerk's lips, Rockefeller turned almost white." Rockefeller asked if he could make a statement and was told he could at the time of his sentencing.

An Alibi Gone Wrong

A week or so earlier in December, Rockefeller had served sixty days in the penitentiary and was released. "Strong efforts were exercised on his behalf to gain his acquittal," the December 30 *Ogden Daily Standard* reported. His brother Jesse testified that he had been with Rockefeller on the day in question, Decoration Day, May 30. But the Union Pacific Railroad record books showed otherwise. Jesse, who worked as a switchman for the railroad, had left the city that day to work as a brakeman on an eastbound train. And then he ran and ran until, while working as a switchman at the depot in Glenns Ferry, Idaho, somebody who knew somebody said to someone that he was working at the Glenns Ferry depot. Jesse must have been surprised when Sheriff Bailey stepped from the train early Sunday morning and arrested him.

Speaking from the county jail in Ogden, Jesse said he could have been "knocked over with a rye straw when the sheriff stepped off the train and said, 'Hello, Jesse,'" the December 30 *Ogden Daily Standard* reported. He thought Glenn's Ferry would be the "last place on earth where he'd be found." He was charged with perjury.

Postscript

The Chinese farmer may have spent some time in jail—or paid a fine. John V. Rockefeller may never have returned to court. Years later, on March 1, 1910, Mary Barnard was arrested for drunkenness. She pleaded guilty, was given a suspended sentence of twenty days and agreed to leave town. The last we know, the two girls, Lizzie and Mary, were remanded to the Crittenton Home, where it's possible they gave up the business of street walking.

Was this the end of the story? Is the case closed? Maybe.

MOTHER URBAN

PARK CITY'S SERIOUSLY ACTIVE RED-LIGHT

In a February 17, 1911 letter that was printed in the *Park Record*, a writer found praise for Park City doctors who, after years of being overworked and underpaid, requested an increase in patient visiting fees. The writer expressed that those owing "get on to themselves, then walk into the doctor's office and hand him [the] few dollars they owe him, lo, these many years." One notable physician lauded by the writer was Dr. LeCompte:

> *Never has a doctor been more attentive than Dr. LeCompte. I have called him hundreds of times to come over and see some unfortunate women of the underworld, and unlike some other doctors, he did not ask me who was going to pay him…but would come immediately and render all assistance possible.*

If an ailing person couldn't pay, the good doctor took it upon himself to make do and "even furnished the medication." In conclusion, Mrs. Rachel B. Urban, destined to be Park City's most intriguing and committed brothel keeper, penned, "This doctor has more consideration for the poor man's family than his pocketbook."

PARK CITY, A STATE IN AND OF ITSELF

Long before Park City, located some thirty-plus miles east of Salt Lake City, became a mountain destination, unrivaled for its world-class downhill and cross-country skiing, the 2002 Olympics and the Sundance Film Festival; long before myriad forest trees, snow and trails flanked cosmopolitan resorts; before there were multicultural restaurants, western art stores, jewelry and fashion boutiques, chocolate shops and down-to-earth saloons; even before the area became a tourist mecca, a recreational wonderland for fly fishers and hikers drawn into nature's beatific wonderment and silence and those hundred-fold history buffs seeking old-time guided silver mine tours and tales; and before the hand-colored printed maps depicted miles and miles of tunnels that looked like a tangle of warrens where claims, congestion, endurance and danger combusted into booms and busts—long before that, Park City was untamed wilderness, random, boundless, fertile and free.

In 1848, Mormon pioneer and leader Parley P. Pratt explored the area's mountainous terrain and canyons and discovered an area that was compatible with grazing cattle, and he called it Parley's Park City. Mr. Pratt also built a toll road, collecting some $1,500 from travelers as they headed to the California gold fields. When Mormon pioneer George Snyder and his sixth wife and family fell in love with the landscape, its deep woodlands and hills that swelled with lush grasses and wildflowers, they eventually settled in the town and shortened its name to Park City.

But it was in the 1860s, during the Civil War (1861–65), when Union officer Colonel Patrick E. Connor was sent to the Salt Lake Valley with over one thousand California voluntary infantry troops to "establish a 2,500-acre camp [known as Fort Douglas] on the east bench, overlooking Salt Lake City which offer[ed] an excellent vantage point from which to observe the goings-on in the territorial capital," author Jeffrey D. Nichols wrote in the Utah State Historical Society's May 1995 *History Blazer*.[75] The colonel's charge was to secure the federal overland mail route and, fearing the Mormons might position themselves with the Confederacy, ensure the Church of Jesus Christ of Latter-day Saints president Brigham Young's loyalty to the Union.[76]

Connor, a California veteran of mining during the gold rush days, also emboldened his men to search for mineral deposits throughout the Utah Territory, including potential discoveries of precious metals in the mountains designated as the Park City Mining District.

The city's first recorded claim in 1869 was called the Young American Lode. Two years later, James M. Kennedy's discovery of silver ore near Park City established the district's Flagstaff Mine. When an outcropping of a large silver ore vein was accidentally discovered by three Canadian prospectors, it was called the Ontario Mine, sold to George Hearst (the father of William

Hearst) in 1872 for $30,000 and recognized as "the greatest silver mine in the world." In its lifetime, Ontario produced millions of dollars in profits for its owners and investors.

Explorations of silver, gold and lead deposits had become a clarion call for hundreds of male prospectors and miners. While this was hazardous, noxious and labor-intensive work, a great number of these men from around the country (and the world) were married and looking for temporary work; they left behind families and wives, hoping to unearth a future of solvency. A good deal more of these men were young and single. Some were experienced miners. Many were poor, and most, if not all, were non-Mormons.

It was in this environment that Park City's development turned from an agrarian lifestyle of agriculture and grazing, a movement sanctioned by President Brigham Young, whose religious precepts supported the self-sufficient lifestyles and collaborative economies that defined the backbone of Mormon towns and settlements, to the industrial extraction and processing of ore or minerals under the ground. The town quickly became one of Utah's mining industry centers.

Notorious for his derision of Mormons and knowing that President Young was against mining, Connor anticipated the mines would bring in a deluge of outsiders to "dilute" the Mormon population with the Park City's diverse cultures, traditions, fraternal organizations and religious affiliations.

The city grew, the mines bloomed like cascades of wildflowers and fortunes were made and lost. According to Captain Jim Balance of the California Center for Military History, State Military Reserve, General Connor, who eventually settled in Utah, established the daily newspaper called the *Utah Vedette* to highlight the state's vigorous mining activity, wrote Utah's early mining laws and founded the mining town of Stockton in the foothills of Oquirrh mountains near the city of Tooele.[77] The general was soon heralded as the father of Utah mining.

In the 1880s, Park City was a boomtown. Its streets were lively; its wood-framed buildings were filled with businesses, shops, housing, mine offices, mills, livery stables and butcher shops, eating establishments, theaters and twenty-three "well patronized" saloons. The town had so many watering holes, in fact, that drunks were aplenty and routinely charged thirty dollars in fines or thirty days in jail. And like most western mining towns, prostitutes arrived early and brothels sprouted, and Park City's red-light district prospered with life lived on the grittier side of town.[78]

MOTHER URBAN AND PARK CITY'S SERIOUSLY ACTIVE RED-LIGHT DISTRICT

Rachel Beulah Hayden was born to Irish immigrants who most likely sailed to America to escape Ireland's devastating Great Famine (1845–55). Onboard mind-numbing, claustrophobic and over-crowded "coffin" ships, thousands of poorly nourished Irish immigrants succumbed to infection and disease and were buried at sea in watery unmarked graves. Rachel's parents were fortunate and survived the trip. They settled in Cleveland, Ohio. By 1846, the Irish represented 10 percent of Cleveland's population of thirteen thousand. The connecting Ohio and Erie Canals offered many work opportunities. Rachel's father may have been employed, but like most new immigrants, he faced discrimination, lower wages and exploitation.

By the time Rachel was twenty-five years old, she had been married and divorced and had a child named Florence. If she was uneducated and poor, with no familial or child support, she might have worked as a prostitute. Arriving in Park City's fast-moving, aggressive mining community in 1889, it is unclear whether she was deeply immersed in the business of prostitution from the outset, had previously established connections in Park City or climbed the ladder and joined the ranks befitting a brothel or parlor madam.

Mother Urban on her porch with her favorite pets, circa the 1920s–1933. *Photograph courtesy of the Park City Historical Society and Museum, Raye Ringholz Collection.*

Mother Urban's "row" of one-room houses for her girls. *Photograph courtesy of the Park City Historical Society and Museum, Bea Kummer Collection.*

By the 1890s, Park City had become one of the five Utah cities and towns to light up its streets with electricity, and it had an escalating population of some five thousand mostly single men, families and few single women. Rachel met local Parkite George Urban, a skilled carpenter, prospector and respected mine owner originally from Copenhagen, Denmark. Nine years later, the couple married and built a well-seasoned and robust business, satisfying the carnal needs of single and lonely miners, trainmen and vast numbers of multifarious, prominent and discreetly anonymous others.

Park City's early red-light stimulus resonated in town near the train station, with "cribs" on the upper floors of local businesses, until the city's residents protested that such houses of ill repute were too close to town, businesses and homes. In 1907, the city's fathers forced the red-light district's soiled doves to move farther east along Heber Avenue (now Deer Valley Drive).

Rachel Urban owned sixteen side-by-side houses that were built by her husband, George, along what was called "the row" or "the line." Her own house on 346 Heber Avenue, close to Swede Alley, was called the Purple Parlor. In the Park City Museum's March 23, 2016 *The Way We Were*, Chris McLaws described Urban's home as being decorated with "lace curtains and fancy furniture. Deemed a respectable parlor, one might imagine a piano and piano man, prostitutes writing letters home for illiterate men and miners congregating, mingling, gambling, drinking and visiting with the working girls."[79]

"There was no charge to visit the girls on the main floor," McLaws wrote. "If miners went upstairs, they paid $2.50 [for the encounter]. It was $10.00 to stay the whole night." In 1900, miners working nine-hour shifts either above or below ground earned between $2.50 and $3.00 a day. Most of them lived in company boardinghouses, bunkhouses or in rough shacks built on mountain slopes close to the mines. Extreme lonesomeness and a feverish yearning for some kind of sexual exchange, no matter the cost, held sway.

Larry Warrens, the author of *Park City: Mountain of Treasure*, noted each house on the line "contained a front room for entertaining, a rear room for more intimate entertaining and a red light on the porch, indicating the girls were accepting visitors."[80]

Not So Easy

Popular lore about the origin of the red in red-light districts varies. Brakemen working for the railroad carried red lanterns and hung them at brothels in case they were needed during emergencies. Amsterdam narratives play with the idea that prostitutes with poor hygiene used red lanterns to obscure their facial imperfections, such as scars, rashes and boils, from potential clients. Some brothels used red lanterns like neon signs, signaling they were open for business; although in many high-class parlors, no such signage appeared on the exterior of the house.

Red lines were drawn on city maps and in published guidebooks to designate the legal boundaries of red-light districts. In parlor homes, the use of red on lamp shades, textiles, wallcoverings, draperies and upholstered furniture dramatized seduction, glamor, wit, power, wealth and success, especially when accompanied by features in gold tones. Red lighting also intensified the erotic appearance and evocative attitude of women who plied their trade from provocatively styled rooms and staged "storefronts" to the more sophisticated brothels and parlors.

In Park City, prostitutes were restricted from walking on Main Street. The town believed the girls, their clothing and behavior would scandalize the proper womenfolk. Called Mother Urban by her working girls, Rachel wanted her girls to be educated, civilized, charming, seductive, healthy, clean and beautiful. She must have kept meticulous accounts of how much each girl earned and what they owed her. Although ambiguous dollar figures are often bandied about (half, less, more, et cetera), just how much prostitutes in her care paid the madam out of their work profits, including such necessities as rent and medical treatment, are conceivably secreted in Urban's private account books. Of course, violence, gunfights, assaults and suicides share a common denominator in most red-light districts.

Keeping a low profile rooted in the underworld, Rachel did not want her girls working the streets or causing a ruckus. Those who did were given a one-way train ticket out of town.

"There were busy nights following the twice-a-month paydays at the mines [and periodical] medical checks [of prostitutes] by Dr. E.P. LeCompte," Warrens wrote. Routine visits by officers assigned to the row often brought levies of fines of $15.00 on the madam for operating a house of ill-fame, $7.50 for each of her working girls, who had to be licensed by the city, and $5.00 for those customers caught in raids using their services.

Rachel Urban was private, self-assured and practical and showed a business acumen and instinct that enabled her to run the precarious business of profitability selling sex. Once a month, she'd arrive at city hall and pay hefty fines and taxes without a disparaging word, which bolstered the city coffers, helped kindle the boomtown economy and cast an aura of respectability over her business.

She also gave back to the community by aiding those who had lost their jobs, as well as numbers of those who had been injured on the job. She supported the city's public schools and paid her respects at funerals,

Park City mine workers, 1900. *Photograph used with permission from the Utah State Historical Society.*

oftentimes calling in on those grieving. She hosted an annual Christmas party for single miners, gave candy to switchboard operators and promoted the efforts of the volunteer fire department by catering a generous spread of turkey sandwiches, liquid refreshments and good cheer. Her actions were received as genuine. She also strove to maintain an amiable relationship with the city's residents while accumulating new clientele for her business.

Mother Urban's ability to maintain a calm, low profile, work within the city's political and legal constraints and ensure client confidentiality while keeping abreast of her expenses earned her a modicum of favorable regard among a begrudging society that considered sexual liaisons sinful.

"The miners, at least, viewed the row as a necessity for the town," author Dalton Gackle wrote in "Behind Closed Doors."[81] When a mayor attempted to close the red-light district, "Urban approached the superintendent of the Judge Mine, a single man, and made her case," Gackle explained. A Park City red-light district without working women would cause mayhem in a town in which "mostly single miners" saturated the city's landscape. If there were no red-light district, where would these miners go to fulfill their physical cravings—and at what cost to the miners, the industry and Park City's revenues?

"[Running to Salt Lake City's red-light district for sexual gratification] meant absenteeism for a couple of days out of the week," Gackle concluded, "[which], in turn, meant less ore mined and less profit for mines."

After the superintendent spoke with the city council, the council relented, and the matter was laid to rest in the red-light district, with twenty-five women known as "seamstresses" on the job.

Park City Cemetery No. 27

Mother Urban donated to the poor and needy and took no flak from city officials or working women. She weighed beyond hefty at some two hundred pounds, brandished a wooden leg, walked with a cane and was driven around by a "uniformed driver." She favored a pet parrot that swore at all passersby, was particularly fond of dogs and cats and ran a profitable business well into the 1930s.

Author Colleen Adair Fliedner, in *Stories in Stone: Park City Cemetery*, published in 1995 by Flair Publishing (Cypress, CA), wrote Mrs. Urban "bore a total of six children," five of whom died before 1910. The surviving child, Richard Urban, who died at the age of fifty-seven, was said to be

"Supposedly" Madam Bessie Wheeler's establishment. *Photograph courtesy of the Park City Historical Society & Museum, Kendall Webb Collection.*

buried with his parents. Little or nothing is known or talked about Rachel's daughter Florence.

Rachel Urban died in 1933. She was sixty-nine years old and suffered from stomach cancer. She was buried in the Park City Cemetery, No. 27, at the extravagant cost of $515, so the fact that her name does not appear on the gravestone is perplexing. The memory of this colorful, kind and tough madam, however, remains endearing and enduring in the red-hot sensuous fabric of Park City history.

The sex business continued without her.

13

THE CLEANER

*D*uring my father's lifetime, there was a red-light district on Edison Street between First and Second South Streets in downtown Salt Lake City," Mary Elizabeth Barker Smith recollected in a February 2, 1983 interview.[82]

Born to an interracial family in Salt Lake City in 1906, Mary lived on American Avenue between Second and Third West Streets. "It's [the downtown street] not there anymore," she said. Her father, William, who was born into slavery, was freed when he was around seven years old. Mary's older sister Mignon thought he must have been eighteen years old when he joined the marching drum corps. "My father was from Joplin, Missouri," Mary said. "He was an express man, carrying trunks and things. He had two horses and often would take me with him on different routes." He also had a two-seated surrey "with a fringe on top, as pretty as you've never seen," she added.

Mary's mother, also named Mary, worked at home, taking in laundry. "She'd go to people's houses, get their laundry, bring them back home, wash by hand at night in a round tub with a washboard and, when they were dry, take them to her customers." Mary said her mother moved to Utah "for the [LDS] church but had an uncle here and went to work in [his] restaurant. I finally grew up in the church for about the first thirteen years and wanted to be baptized. But when this lady friend [of my mother's] told me [I'd] never be able to go into the temple, I forgot about it. I didn't get baptized."

Mary's sister Mignon attended Utah State University and is considered the state's first Black college graduate. "I think when she came out of school, she couldn't get a job here [and would have had] to leave town [to find employment]," Mary said, "but she didn't want to leave her family, and so, she took a job as a maid up at the University of Utah in the home economics department."

With support from the faculty, Mignon became involved with the university's Stewart Training School, which was focused on preparing students for careers in teaching. Attended by children from kindergarten through high school, "it was there and because of the kids that my sister started a lunch program for them," Mary said.

Throughout her life—to the accolades of many—Mignon went on to help minority youth groups. The memories of the much younger Mary, though, speak to her early days of enjoying an easy-going childhood and being a kid who just loved school and play.

House of Prostitution and Close to Home

Mary also remembered a specific incident in her life: the time she spent working in a house of prostitution. Although faced with a sparsity of dates, her recall is clear, even when becoming aware of illicit happenings going on in the apartment above her.

"At the time, we were renting a house on Eight South and Fourth East Streets for twenty dollars a month, when the owner suddenly got married." she said. "A woman I worked with in the brothel decided to take the three upstairs bedrooms and make an apartment out of it. So, we had five rooms downstairs, and she had three."

It was an agreeable arrangement, and it seemed all was going well until one Sunday evening, when Mary returned from a show—she simply loved the cinema—and noticed that somebody had been on the back porch, apparently attempting to get into her house. "He must have tried to get around to the back door but couldn't find it, so he broke the glass in our kitchen [window], undid the screw lock and climbed in," she said.

The intruder was drunk, and after breaking in, he started to "ransack the kitchen" before stumbling into a bedroom, where he startled one of Mary's sons, who had been sleeping. Roused awake, the son jumped up, saw the interloper, punched the man's arm and yelled, "What are you doing?" The potential burglar mumbled that he needed to go to the woman who lived upstairs. Startled by the commotion, another son ran into the room and directed the drunkard out of their house and onto the back porch toward an overlooked (second) door by the kitchen with steps that led to the second floor.

"We had both been working in a prostitute house," Mary said, "and I guess she had been working with [different customers] and bringing them to the house. At the time, they used to have prostitution houses all over Salt Lake City. And I guess she was going to try a trick or two on her own."

Mary worked in the brothel on Third South and First West Streets. "There must have been one, two, three, four, five or six rooms upstairs," she recalled. "They had a big living room where the men picked out the girls they wanted to take upstairs with them." Mary and her upstairs neighbor didn't have to cook because food was always brought in, mostly from a café just around the corner. "All we had to do was answer the door, show them into the living room and send the girls in there."

Meeting the madam when she was hired, Mary learned that most of the sex workers had boyfriends. "I guess you could call them pimps," she said, "but none of them were ever allowed to come into the house."

Once a week, the house prostitutes would be examined at the board of health. They were young, "nice-looking girls." The price for sex was one dollar, and one night, only one girl showed up to work. "That woman turned ninety-six tricks," Mary said. "Besides washing dishes, all I was doing was putting a man in her room. She'd come out of that room and go to the next room just like that. We counted them, and [by the end of the night], she made ninety-six dollars."

There were times when Mary would be approached. "One of the men would say, 'How about you?' or something like that. I'd say, 'No way.'"

"There were houses of prostitution all over town," she continued, "I knew a man that bought a house I think near the Elks Club, before the club was there. He just made a hotel out of the house, with rooms upstairs [for prostitutes]. Then there was one down on Second South [Street], just west of West Temple. I think there were two red brick buildings there."

The men would show up but apparently not linger. "It wasn't like they'd stay all evening long," Mary explained. "I think they only allowed them about three minutes in a room with a girl."

Too Much

Mary said it was an easy house to work in. It was never raided. She never had any trouble. "But it had me so upset, I couldn't eat anything." She couldn't touch or bear washing the glasses and plates that came from the rooms. "Just seeing them going to those girls; it was just sickening. I hated myself [for being any part of it]. It was awful—that work—but it was a job, and I think I made thirty-six dollars a week."

Six or seven months later, Mary Smith walked away from cleaning up after the girls and took another job working at downtown Main Street's ZCMI, Zions Cooperative Mercantile Institution, known as the People's Store.

14

THE FIERCELY UNFETTERED
CITY OF OGDEN

Part One: Twenty-Fifth Street

Linda Kunie Oda, née Inouye, must have been around six years old when she first noticed gaming tables, chairs and a tunnel in the dimly lit basement of her parents' Kay's Food Market on 227½ Twenty-Fifth Street in downtown Ogden City.

"It was a small space, and the word was, during Prohibition, it had been a speakeasy," the former director of Asian affairs in the Governor's Office of Ethnic Affairs (2007–11) told this author.[83] Early on, lighting or sound alarm systems were rigged to alert patrons to potential raids, and once warned, "everyone moved quickly through the tunnel to the alley and disappeared," Oda said. "But that was years ago." However, it was truly not forgotten.

Ogden's seeds were sown when nineteen-year-old Miles Goodyear—born in 1817 in Hamden, Connecticut, and soon an orphan—traveled west to experience frontier life. He became a fur trapper, trader and mountain man. After marrying Pomona, the daughter of Chief Peteetneet, the indigenous clan leader of the Timpanogos Ute band, the couple had two children. By 1845, Goodyear had built a trading post called Fort Buenaventura and moved in with his family. At the junction of the Weber and Green Rivers, the mountain man constructed several log cabins, homes, corrals and sheds for other trappers and Natives to inhabit.[84] It was the first permanent white settlement in the Great Basin, and there, Goodyear cultivated a garden and provided services to emigrants on their westward-bound trek to California.

In 1847, LDS president Brigham Young, who laid out street plans for Salt Lake City's development, sent two men, James Brown (one of the city's founders) and Lorin Farr (the city's first mayor), to purchase the small settlement and surrounding land from Goodyear. Already feeling crowded by the influx of pioneer settlers, Goodyear sold the fort to the Mormon High Council for $1,950, a sum later adjusted to be $3,000.

Ogden, named after Hudson Bay Company trapper Peter Skeen Ogden, was incorporated in 1851. Lorin Farr founded the town's gristmills and sawmills. Pioneer David Burch established a wheat mill along the Weber River. And in the mid-1880s, entrepreneur David Eccles introduced his lumber mill. The Kuhn brothers ran wholesale dry goods and clothing enterprises. In 1889, industry developer Frederick J. Kiesel became the city's first gentile (Jewish) mayor, enhancing the sociological diversity of the city's population. And on the outskirts of town, Japanese farmers cultivated sweetheart celery and world-renowned everbearing strawberries.

There's no mistaking the jump-start that spurred Ogden's rapid development. In 1869, when the nation's first transcontinental railroad rolled into Union Station (eventually with terminals for nine different railway systems), the town mushroomed into an accommodating, hard-hitting railroad town. Called Junction City for the Union and Central Pacific Railroads, the once-agricultural town became a major transportation link and a magnet for the tourist trade. Directly across the street from Union depot, the Wild West red-light district of Two-Bit Street rolled out the red carpet. Its residents raised the curtains on the subterranean tunnels that bestrode vice above and below street level. Tucked between and above legal businesses, working women catered to men.

"When you've got guns, girls or whiskey, it doesn't take a lot of imagination to figure out what to do with a network of tunnels and underground rooms," Scott Vanleeuwen told this author during a visit to his gift shop, Ogden's oldest pawnshop on Twenty-Fifth Street.

Descending a steep set of stairs in his shop, we walked into a reconstructed dirt cellar and passed a wall-mounted regiment of rifles and some exquisitely hand-tooled saddles. Off to a dark and dusty side, he headed toward what one might think is another building; instead, it was a boarded-up door with an alarm that stood out from the residue fragments of a raucous and lawless past beckoning to be remembered.

Amid myriad rumors about the underground tunnels and their existence—ostensibly built for running hooch, creating opium dens, setting up gambling clubs or engaging working women—this author turned to a

248 DAVENPORT BUILDING   252 LONDON ICE CREAM PARLOR

SOUTH ELEVATION

OGDEN'S 25TH STREET 2

Ogden's Twenty-Fifth Street façade. *Drawing by Chad Nielsen; photograph courtesy of Thomas Carter.*

friend, longtime Ogdenite and history bloodhound Robin Macnofsky, for clarification. She replied:

> *As a writer/editor (1998–2001) for* Northern Utah Junction *magazine, marketing manager in 2002 for Peery's Egyptian Theater, and arts coordinator for Ogden City from 2002–2007, I had many opportunities to speak with business owners on Twenty-Fifth Street about the legendary "tunnels" rumored to run from Union Station up three historic blocks of Twenty-Fifth Street to Peery's Egyptian Theater located on Washington Blvd.*
>
> *On one occasion, I accompanied Dan Musgrave, executive director of Downtown Ogden Inc. as we explored the basement of a business located on the north side of the 200 block. There was a door on the south-facing basement wall, which opened into a narrow subterranean "alley"*

256-260 UNION RESTAURANT BUILDING   264-266 PORTER BLOCK BUILDING

BLOCK COMMERCIAL DISTRICT

approximately four feet wide and barely six inches in height, laying directly below the paved sidewalk. This rough-hewn alley (also known as a tunnel) spanned the length of the basement and [was] bricked off on each east and west end.

The owner explained that since coal was the primary source of heating fuel when the buildings were constructed, metal chutes funneled coal deliveries from the street into the subterranean alley. Business owners would shovel the piles of coal through their basement door to feed their furnace. Once Twenty-Fifth Street transitioned to electricity in the 1890s (also known as Electric Alley), the chutes were converted to freight lifts, and eventually, the openings were permanently sealed with glass blocks.

"It is reasonable," Macnofsky concluded, "that this 'coal' alley would have run along the north and south length of Twenty-Fifth Street and, at one time, been connected to the basement of Peery's Egyptian Theater. There is still a portion of this alley under the theater, which is known to flood on occasion when the water table under the city rises due to rapid spring snow melt. The mythical stories of opium dens and gambling clubs in the Twenty-Fifth Street alleys are also reasonable, given the secretive and protected nature of these spaces, where such illicit pursuits would be left undisturbed."

Rumors leached into Ogden's, sometimes called "Little Chicago's," narrative when the undisputed emperor of Chicago Al Capone got off the train at Union Station sometime in the 1920s and walked up Twenty-Fifth Street, seeking business opportunities—bootlegging, prostitution, gambling—for the mob. Although it's difficult to believe, anecdotes erupted that after running into full-scale corruption on the notorious street, which was also marked for shootings and all manners of violence, the prohibition-era czar called Scarface fled on the next train out of town, saying the area was too rough for him. Another unfounded tale persists that Mr. Capone found sanctuary, hiding from the feds for weeks on end, in Ogden.

Serving an eleven-year sentence for federal tax evasion at the Atlantic U.S. Penitentiary in 1931 and then being transferred to Alcatraz, the most feared man suffered from late-stage paresis (partial paralysis), possibly having contracted syphilis early on, which later caused inflammation in his brain. Deteriorating, Capone was released early from prison into the care of his truly devoted wife, Mae. Capone was treated with medicinal drugs of the time, but the heralded cure-all, penicillin, wasn't developed for distribution in America until 1943, and at first, it was only distributed in limited supply. When Mr. Capone, who may have been in a temporary remission stage for several years, received penicillin treatment, it was too late. He was already profoundly deteriorating. In 1947, Capone (who detested his nickname, Scarface) suffered a stroke, caught pneumonia and died.[85]

Until World War II, lawlessness, bootlegging, gambling halls, brothels, opium dens, saloons, speakeasies (called iron door clubs), corruption, prostitution and depravity swelled in the bawdy parts on and around Two-Bit Street.

On this very street, the first to be paved in Ogden in 1885, a handsome array of turn-of-the-century architecture housed legitimate businesses, stores, hotels, taverns, underground tunnels and many red-light persuasions embodied in second-floor brothels and cribs. All are richly woven into the historic fabric of Ogden's rebellious early history.

Whether those underground tunnels that thrived on dodgy doings and criminal activity are imagined myths or forgotten truths, Ogden's encounter with the underworld's immorality remains avidly embraced by some and is certainly difficult to shrug off.

Part Two: Belle London and Her Prostitution Syndicate

Much like the Old West, even before the arrival of the transcontinental railroad, Ogden's fortitude and pockets of grittiness were a magnet for madams seeking fertile ground for houses of ill repute. And there were many, according to Val Holley, who lists prominent brothel keepers, such as "Aunt" Fanny Payne, who, in a scuffle with a rival, Madam Ida Abels, shot at her, and she shot back, resulting in both being arrested, taken to court and fined fifty dollars, and Maggie Kirk, who swore she ran a proper boardinghouse, although police raids discovered opium trappings under bedsheets and she was later charged with operating a brothel and opium den.[86]

Arguably, one of Ogden's most notorious madams who commanded sustainability, know-how and a modicum of respect was Belle London. Born in Kentucky or Illinois, her birthname might have been Dora Bella Hughes. According to historian Jan MacKell in *Red Light Women of the Rocky Mountains*, the razor-sharp woman was known as Dora Topham in 1890 after marrying and twice attempting to divorce Union Pacific boilermaker and barkeep Thomas Topham. During this time, she gave birth to a daughter named Ethel (although her daughter may have been adopted).[87] While the couple managed to work together on successful business ventures, they led mostly separate lives, apparently loaded with issues.

A rough man and owner of the busy Mint Saloon with a reputation of never walking away from a fight, Topham was several years into his marriage when he was accused of murdering a man, "a cigar maker, Charles Wessler," wrote Holley, "who [came into the bar] and asked him to repay an old bill. Topham suggested taking it out in drinks." The men argued until Topham knocked down Wessler and jumped on him with his feet again and again. As to who did what to whom, testimonies from the customers who jumped into the fracas were conflicting. Two days later, Wessler died. Charged with murder, Topham was hauled into court but was acquitted. "But his involvement in the incident may have been the beginning and end of his marriage to Dora," MacKell wrote.

Belle London. *Photograph used with permission from the Utah State Historical Society.*

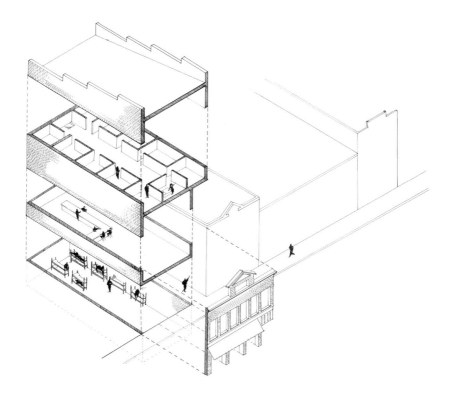

The Davenport Saloon building once housed an opium den (in the basement), the saloon (on the first floor) and brothels (on the second floor). *Drawing by Chad Nielsen; photograph courtesy of Thomas Carter.*

Petitioning to resume using her maiden name, Dora was mostly identified as Belle London, the "queen of Ogden's underworld." The woman looked more like a thoughtful librarian than a female procuress. And yet, in the Victorian era, that look still dominated American culture and social mores in the late 1800s, especially as successful women in the realm of male-run businesses were rarities. London operated a large prostitution syndicate.

Arriving in Ogden from Denver, Colorado, in 1889, London wasted no time getting into the city's real estate boom and building up a lucrative yet immoral business. She acquired and operated private parlors, legal shops, bordellos and other real estate assets. Understood to be the first owner of the Davenport Saloon, where she established brothels in the floors above, she maintained enough rooming houses and second-story brothels to occupy a large portion of the buildings in the 200 block on Twenty-Fifth Street. In one such venture, the woman proprietress, who owned the Star Lunch Room in the present-day London Ice Cream Parlor location at 252–54 Twenty-Fifth Street, advertised her business in the *Ogden City Directory* and was described in part by author Lyle J. Barnes in his book *Notorious Two-Bit Street*:

> *"Open Day and Night. Everything First Class in the Season.…Newly Furnished and Well-Ventilated Rooms in Connection. Private Dining Rooms Upstairs."* This was a very unusual lunchroom—open every day. Certainly, it was more than a "lunchroom" type of business.[88]

While London may have advertised her business with bold finesse, knowing full well her name alone summoned customers, she was protective of her young daughter's anonymity and insisted on discretion. So, when it came to her daughter's education, in need of a tutor, London's chauffeur would drive Ethel to the teacher's home in the madam's recognizable horse-drawn surrey, stop a block away from the educator's house and let Ethel out to walk the rest of the way. After class, Ethel would backtrack to the same spot on the block, where she'd find the chauffeur waiting to take her home—and no one would be the wiser that the young girl was Madam London's daughter.

Belle London paid her fines and those of her girls, some of whom listed their occupations as music teacher, seamstress and artist. She spoke out for other brothel keepers and rented them houses or parlors. And she effectively wrangled with city commissioners, police officials, lawyers, judges, architects, businessmen and others among Ogden's elite. Many who disparaged or begrudged her in public respected her profitable business acumen as they would a man's and were willing to do business with her under the mantle of Ogden's fierce independence, even when such transactions were censured by their religious affiliations and parties. Business is business.

Licentious sex, alcohol, gambling, saloons and lewd activities that catered to lascivious conduct were egregious affronts to Mormon morality. Yet many saloons on Twenty-Fifth Street were owned and operated by Mormons. Part-owners of the boisterous White Elephant Saloon and Gambling Hall, which could accommodate several hundred patrons, the Stephens brothers' reputations as builders went back to the Mormon temple in Nauvoo, Illinois (dedicated in 1846), and the buildings on Twenty-Fifth Street.

"Mormon ownership also complicated public debate on Ogden's variety theaters," wrote Val Holley. The Stephens brothers' Novelty Theatre's profits were more likely to come when "female rustlers peddled alcohol and cigars to men in the audience, particularly those who sat in private boxes in the balcony."[89]

The White Elephant Saloon. *Photograph used with permission from the Utah State Historical Society.*

Both the Novelty Theater and Richard James Taylor and David Kay's Lyceum Theatre were lambasted by the *Deseret News*, which insisted "bolder and more brazen dens of vice never existed in Sodom and Gomorrah." Yet the real estate Belle London needed to build Electric Alley was purchased from well-known Mormon businessman David H. Peery Jr.[90]

By 1902, London saw an opportunity to expand her prostitution consortium in the alley just behind Twenty-Fifth Street. Creating a walkway between the Davenport Saloon (246–48 Twenty-Fifth Street) and the London Ice Cream Parlor building (252–54 Twenty-Fifth Street) that led into the alley, she hired the Stephens brothers (for some $10,000) to build much of the housing in what became Electric Alley, an extravaganza of sexual pleasure and more.

Ogden's 1906 Sanborn fire insurance maps clearly show the scattered rows of cribs flanking the alley's entrance along the rear of Twenty-Fifth Street,

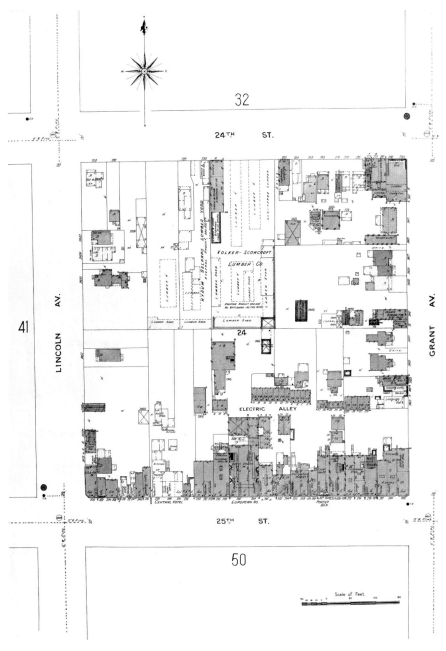

Ogden's Electric Alley, Sanborn map detail. *Courtesy of the Special Collections, J. Willard Marriott Library, University of Utah.*

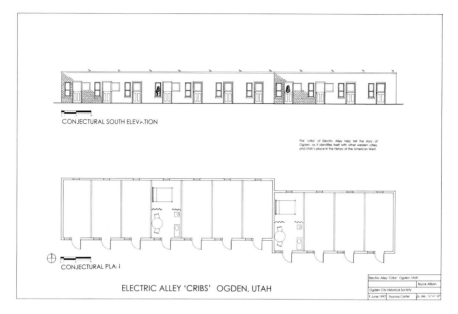

CONJECTURAL SOUTH ELEVATION

The 'cribs' of Electric Alley help tell the story of
Ogden, as it identifies itself with other western cities,
and Utah's place in the history of the American West.

CONJECTURAL PLAN

ELECTRIC ALLEY 'CRIBS' OGDEN, UTAH

Electric Alley 'Cribs' Ogden, Utah		
		Bryce Allison
Ogden City Historical Society		
9 June 1997	Thomas Carter	Scale: ¼"=1'-0"

Electric Alley cribs. *Drawings by Bryce Allison; photograph courtesy of Thomas Carter.*

with more positioned within the alley's parameters, and each of the fifty or so tiny domiciles is labeled "F.B." for "female boarder." Women stood in their front doors or by the windows of their eight-by-eight-foot dwellings to lure, cajole, coax and invite customers to come in. Parlor houses—some run by other madams—were also built by London and filled with six to eight inmates.

Belle London's large and stunning No. 10 Electric Alley parlor house, staffed with a butler, cook and beautiful women, "glittered" (was maybe even electrified) with masquerade balls and lavish late dinners. After originally inviting the public to these dinners, London later denied women who arrived without invitations.

Once a month, the police would arrive to arrest or fine London and her prostitutes for keeping a house of ill repute. Paying five dollars for each of her workers and fifteen for herself, London would record it as a "normal business expense."

For all Electric Alley's flashiness and appeal, there were pockets of vice and corruption, where attempted murders, suicides, larceny and pilfering pervaded. A parlor called the Ice Palace (renovated in an abandoned three-room rookery), run by "Hog-Faced Mag" and "Queen Lil," was notorious for its "holdups and other atrocities." It was so dreadful, the police shuttered it within a month.

One must wonder if city officials were paid to look the other way for Electric Alley to have even been built and boldly exist. Both the illicit goings-on of Twenty-Fifth Street and Electric Alley itself were recognized in Utah and neighboring states. Junction City was the stopover for jazz and vice between Colorado and California, and it was known to travelers well in advance of their rolling into Union Station.

"Elder Browning's Protected 'Red-Light' in Ogden"

The newspaper editorial sounded like a bellowing, unrelenting bullhorn, its outraged banner blasting accusations above its exposed body copy. Protected red-light district? Depraved women? Nepotism? Churchmen involvement? Accompanying a pictorial disclosure of Electric Alley, the October 21, 1908 *Salt Lake Tribune*, on page 8, divulged a seething truth:

> [H]*erewith is a fair portrayal of the red-light district in Ogden, which is controlled by the notorious Belle London. There is nothing like it in the intermountain country. The habitues of these little whitewashed "cribs" are the lowest type of depraved women to be found on earth. Their conduct is so revolting that it would be impossible to describe it.*
>
> *Every one of these poor creatures is compelled to contribute a considerable percent of her earnings to Belle London. This woman has grown rich from this awful white slavery. The Ogden chief of police is an active elder in the Mormon Church. This officer recently discharged three Catholic policemen from the force to make way for three Mormons, whom he could better control. Such protection as Chief* [Thomas E.] *Browning gives to Belle London enables her to control absolutely the prostitution of Junction City.*

Without a breath spared, the *Salt Lake Tribune* leaned into its allegations: "Chief Browning insists the women 'repair' to his relative Dr. W.J. Browning's office 'at regular internal to obtain from the young doctor a certificate of health.' And that the public is left in the dark about the chief's strategy, as Belle London's working girls 'go deeper into their shame to earn this shameless fee.'"

Then, changing course to expose more of the ongoing rift in prevailing religious efficacies, admonished the *Deseret News*, which:

> *has not a word of rebuke to its elder of the Weber Stake of Zion, who permits and protects Belle London to carry on this awful traffic in the*

Left: Ogden Chief of police Thomas. E. Browning. *Photograph courtesy of the Special Collections, Stewart Library, Weber State University.*

Below: Moral upset blares from the October 21, 1908 *Salt Lake Tribune*. *Photograph courtesy of the Special Collections, J. Willard Marriott Library, University of Utah.*

ELDER BROWNING'S PROTECTED "RED LIGHT" IN OGDEN

souls and bodies of her white slaves. Is there any wonder Salt Lakers are
disgusted with the "reform" policy of the church politicians here when it is
known what a system is protected by high churchmen in Ogden?

Earlier, in December 1906, charges of dereliction of duty were made against the chief, and many demanded that he be removed from office. The following January, the case was thrown out of court.

The Reputation They Desired

Whatever might be said to despoil Belle London's reputation, first and foremost in the minds of some Salt Lake authorities was her enduring and extraordinary business prowess and how it might have benefited their city that was run amok with prostitution. It was not long before they came calling.

THE CORRALLING OF WOMEN

You never used your own name in hustling. I used a different name practically every week. If you got busted, it was more difficult for them to find out who you really were. The role one plays has nothing to do with who you are. It's only fitting and proper you take another name....As a bright, assertive woman, I had no power. As a cold manipulative hustler, I had a lot.
—*Roberta, from call girl to drug-addled streetwalker before coming clean*[91]

LARGE HAULS

By the 1870s, Salt Lake City's downtown red-light district was feisty, rip-roaring and out of control. Evenings in the district's Commercial Street, Plum Alley, Franklin Avenue and Victoria Place were, by reputation, tailored for the madding crowds of customers from high-hats to everyday Joes searching and willing to pay for pleasure.

This is not to say the police force was inefficient. Officers conducted raids. Judges ordered fines. Brothel madams paid monthly fines for operating houses of ill repute and for each of her working girls, stoking the city coffers (sometimes as much as $1,500 every month) in an ambivalent symbiotic relationship. Physical examinations were sometimes given. Unlucky girls were scurried into jail. Street workers, who were most often at risk of abuse and among the poorest in the sex trade, worked on their own or were harnessed by pimps and police; they struggled to survive. Some just disappeared from the streets. Others left, only to return under an assumed name.

Clearly, the illegal but tolerated prostitution business had a foothold in the city, with extraordinary amounts of money (in fines and contributions) going, as you know by now, to city taxes—"an important part of the city's revenues"—or into the pockets of others. The profession also seemed impervious to all attempts to curtail—let alone abolish—it. There was profitable business to be had in Salt Lake City, and numbers of city residents (and legitimate business owners) were appalled; and the police reacted with a series of raids.

"The police have made a huge haul last night after the serving of warrants on gamblers and prostitutes," the August 8, 1894 *Salt Lake Tribune* reported. "Six gamblers chipped in $50.00 each. Helen Blazes, Gisele Blake, Addie O'Nell, Essie Waters and Melvina Beauchamp, keepers of houses of ill fame, were requested to put up $17.00 each and the 'boarders,' forty-six in all, left $8.50 each." Within a few short years, these fines were increased to $50.00 or even $100.00.

Such efforts did not curb the wayward women's activities, quash rumors that city officials had financial stakes in buildings that housed female boarders or mollify respectable residents' growing displeasure.

Among the buildings on Commercial Street, the heart of the red-light district closest to downtown businesses, historian John S. McCormick wrote that there were those built by Utah's "leading citizens," who, like "those throughout the United States, commonly owned land and buildings in the red-light districts."[92]

In 1893, Gustavus S. Holmes, a National Bank of the Republic director and owner of the Knutsford Hotel, "constructed two buildings on Commercial Street" between Third South and State Streets. While legitimate businesses, like cigarette and magazine shops, print shops, cafés and saloons operated on the first floor of each building, prostitutes (or female boarders) could be found sitting in a parlor house on the second floor, welcoming customers and attending to their needs in any one of the eight-by-ten-foot cribs (which commonly had a bed, chair and washstand) that flanked the public space. On that same notorious street, known for its decadence and delight, another National Bank of the Republic director and "real estate speculator," Stephen Hayes, also had a building designed by the notable architect Walter E. Ware (whose work has been listed in the National Register of Historic Places). And for some time, Salt Lake City Council member Martin E. Mulvey, who was purported to be a gambler, ran a saloon on the first floor and was instrumental in planning what became known as the stockade.

In the January 4, 1895 *Salt Lake Tribune*, Salt Lake City police chief Arthur Pratt suggested prostitutes be confined "in one locality":

> *The evil cannot be suppressed, but it must be restrained and kept under strict police control. It is a more difficult problem to handle when the women are scattered out than when they are kept together.*

By the 1900s, deportment parted waters, as the town's gentry reached a boiling point and, seething with anger, demanded the city rid itself of prostitutes. Their presence was harming respectable businesses, driving away potential customers, raising rents in the area and disturbing the neighborhood ambiance with crowded, noisy, dangerous and offensive carryings-on.

The notion of purging Commercial Street of prostitutes was seen as "commendable" but not necessarily practical. It was a topic that would not dissipate for those who were adversely affected by the lascivious goings-on in their neighborhood.

According to McCormick, LDS church leader Nephi W. Clayton wrote that the *Deseret News* favored a "restricted red-light district built on the far west side of the city," while the *Salt Lake Tribune* supported a middle ground, creating a new street "into the interior of some of the downtown blocks." Most residents and businessmen alike realized the futility of attempting to eliminate the incursion of prostitutes. By then, the red-light district was already spreading out, with brothels opening on Main and Brigham Streets, Helen Blazes's new parlor opening on Seventh South and Main Streets and secret dens emerging uptown.

SOMETHING HAD TO BE DONE

Mayor John Bransford (1907–12) and the Salt Lake City Council, comprised of male representatives from fifteen different districts and several political parties, including members of the anti-Mormon American Party—Bransford himself was a member of the American and Democratic Parties and was respected by Saints and gentiles—knew a change had to be made.[93] The oft-mentioned notion of a stockade occupied much secular and spiritual thought in Zion.

In 1907, Police Chief Thomas D. Pitt, newly appointed by the Salt Lake City mayor, proposed the red-light district be moved to a less-intrusive area of the city. Building a stockade surrounded by high walls and cottages for prostitutes to rent while working under the control of the police department and the board of health would help relieve the ongoing afflictions created by their presence downtown. The selling points to Pitt's proposition included sanitation, safety, cleanliness, confinement and control.

Working together across divergent views and reaching a consensus, "Mayor John Bransford and the Salt Lake Council accepted Pitt's recommendation," wrote McCormick, "and in the spring of 1908, began to plan the stockade." They needed investors, a place to build and someone to manage the build and run the affair.

BLOCK 64

In the western edge of the city, Block 64 (100–200 South Street and 500–600 West Street), near the railroad tracks, was, by the early 1900s, also home to an enclave of hardworking Greek and Italian immigrants who, distinguished Greek American ethnographer Helen Papanikolis wrote, "were stunned by the hate of Americans. 'The scum of Europe,' 'depraved brutal foreigners,' they were called in print."[94] Such rank discrimination fouling the minds of enough committee members, officials and others made Block 64 an obvious solution.

WHO'S RUNNING THE SHOW?

Jeffrey Nichols wrote that although eminent Salt Lake City madams, such as "Emma DeMarr, Helen Blazes, Ada Wilson, and Beatrice 'Bee' Bartlett," had been operating houses with the connivance of the authorities," they were not considered for the vacant position.[95]

But the notorious Belle London, the queen of the Ogden underworld, who saturated the city's Twenty-Fifth Street (among others) with business, brothels and cribs—the same woman equipped with the business acumen to astonish the most astute of businessmen; that illegal madam who singularly raised enough money to build, own and rent out cribs, set up parlors and brighten the illicit corners of Electric Alley; that woman, Mrs. Dora B. Topham, with a list of fiscal accomplishments—must have astounded the Salt Lake councilmen and the mayor, who, with Mulvey, came courting. "Bransford and Mulvey asked her to form a corporation, purchase land on

Salt Lake's west side in the center of Block 64…and set up and operate a stockade," wrote McCormick.

Belle London agreed, and later, in reflection, she told the *Salt Lake Tribune* (September 28, 1911):

> *I know and you know that prostitution has existed since the earlier ages, and if you are honest with yourselves, you will admit that it will continue to exist, no matter what may be said or done from the pulpit or through the exertions of women's clubs. I believed that I could segregate the evil, that I could control it and I could decrease disease by intelligent management and, while profiting financially myself, do some good in this city.*

She also spoke of her successful work in Ogden that she said she wanted accomplished for the women of the stockade:

> *It may not be generally known, but it is a fact that I have maintained a hospital at Ogden…where all women under my charge in need of treatment have been cared for. I have endeavored to persuade girls who were not yet beyond saving to lead the lives they should lead, and sometimes, I have succeeded.*

Moral outrage about the stockade shouted from the September 23, 1908 *Deseret Evening News. Photograph used with permission from the Utah State Historical Society.*

During the summer of 1908, London formed the Citizen's Investment Company to purchase the land of Block 64. According to the U.S. Department of the Interior and the National Park Services' Register of Historic Places, London "served as president, treasurer and general manager of the company, controlling 2,460 of the 2,500 shares. The Salt Lake Security and Trust Company was granted a trust deed for $200,000 and provided the necessary capital for the land purchase and construction."

As the stockade was being built, the September 23, 1908 *Deseret Evening News*, which had remained mum on Ogden's Electric Alley when accusations were pitted against an active LDS member and chief of police who purportedly provided protection to Belle London, sardonically blared aspersions against the American Party as the root of the stockade's existence.

City Councilman L.D. Martin was selected as the architect. In September, construction began. By December, the brick-and-mortar stockade was completed, with electrically wired alarms installed to warn of incoming raids.

The Stockade and Its Women

Surrounded by a ten-foot-tall, two-door, gated wall, the stockade housed 150 segregated ten-foot-by-ten-foot cribs, large brothels rented from London by landladies for $175 a month, boardinghouses, a dancehall, a saloon, opium dens, restaurants, a storehouse for beer and liquor and related businesses on the perimeter.

Each crib, rented nightly to prostitutes for one to four dollars a day, was a ten-foot-square room with a door and window in front for the woman to call out to customers. Divided by curtains, each crib included a washstand with a chair placed in front and an enameled bed in the back.

While celebratory music, food and possibly liquor were brought out in force for the opening of the stockade, from the start, the stockade had its own woes, including secret entrances, corruption, bribes, raids and deals. Inmates were forced to buy from company stores and reside in nearby company-owned homes. Even when London offered potential inmates a week of free board and room in her brothel, emphasizing the safety and protection, the concept of being in a pen was a struggle.

"Topham offered houses to several established madams, including Cleo Starr, a keeper at 222 South State Street; Madge Daniels of the Palace; Lou Sheppard, a Commercial Street veteran; Irene McDonald of Commercial

Opposite, top: Clearing the land for the stockade. *Photograph used with permission from the Utah State Historical Society.*

Opposite, bottom: Constructing one long row of cribs. *Photograph used with permission from the Utah State Historical Society.*

Above: Workmen between the cribs. *Photograph used with permission from the Utah State Historical Society.*

Street and Topham's Ogden brothels; Rose Bartlett of 243 South Main Street," wrote Nichols. "All but Sheppard accepted the offer."[96] Reluctant madams and independent streetwalkers were strongarmed into either transferring to the stockade or getting out of town. While some in the business of prostitution might have left, others did not relocate.

For myriad reasons, there was vigorous opposition of outraged west side residents who felt pressed to live between the active railroad and the overwhelmingly and dangerous stockade, similar to the reaction of downtown city residents who were adversely affected by their red-light district. Disgruntlement trumpeted in newspapers, and fractious blame tarnished the participating public officials. Belle London, who left the

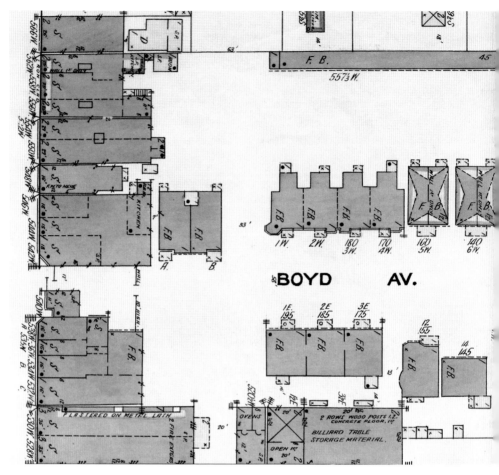

Sanborn map, 1911, with cribs for prostitutes straddling Boyd Avenue in the stockade. *Photograph courtesy of the Special* Collections, *J. Willard Marriott Library, University of Utah.*

stockade and returned to Ogden, faced charges of "pandering," leading to a sentence of "eighteen years of hard labor." Of course, after some twenty-two years in the business of prostitution and garnering respect for her business acumen (and possibly having a black book filled with names), the charges were dropped.

The stockade closed for good in 1911. But prostitution in the city survived into the…well, business is business.

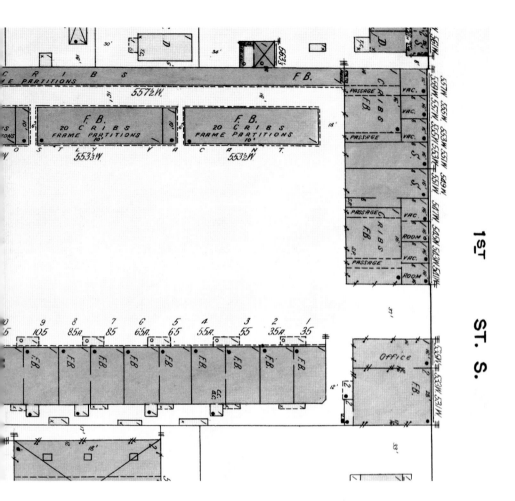

NOTES

Chapter 1

1. Alford and Freeman, "Salt Lake Theater"; Andrew Jenson, *Encyclopedic History of the Church of Jesus Christ of Latter-day Saints* (Salt Lake City, UT: Deseret News, 1941), 762.
2. Kenneth L. Alford and Robert C. Freeman, "The Salt Lake Theatre: Brigham's Playhouse," in *Salt Lake City: The Place Which God Prepared*, edited by Scott C. Esplin and Kenneth L. Alford (Provo, UT: BYU Religious Studies Center and Deseret Book, 2011), 107–8. https://scholarsarchive. byu.edu/cgi/viewcontent.cgi?article=2728&context=facpub.
3. Official Report of the Semi-Annual General Conference of the Church of Jesus Christ of Latter-day Saints, 1911, *Salt Lake City*, in "Appreciating a Pretty Shoulder," 140–41.
4. Campbell, *Johnson and the Erotic Mormon Image*, 8–9.
5. Davis, "Appreciating a Pretty Shoulder," 123.
6. Campbell, *Johnson and the Erotic Mormon Image*, 9.
7. Ibid., 9–10.
8. Davis, "Appreciating a Pretty Shoulder," 132.
9. Ibid., 143.

Chapter 2

10. William H. Gonzalez and Orlando Rivera, "Hispanics of Utah," *Utah History Encyclopedia*, https://www.uen.org/utah_history_encyclopedia/h/HISPANICS_OF_UTAH.shtml.

11. The Territory of Utah, an organized incorporated territory of the United States, existed from 1850 to 1896, when Utah, reduced to is present borders, was admitted to the union as the forty-fifth state. In 1861 and 1866, Nevada became a separate territory; Colorado separated from Utah in 1861; Montana separated from Utah in 1861; and Wyoming separated in 1868. The annexation of Texas, in 1845, was bitterly rejected by Mexico, which considered the territory part of Mexico. This added to the 1846 armed conflict.

12. There was such a dearth of hospitals in the western frontier, it wasn't until 1872 that St. Marks Hospital became the first hospital to open in Salt Lake City; while some five hundred miles away, St. Mary Louise Hospital, in 1875, served Virginia City, Nevada, a former part of the incorporated Utah Territory.

13. For varying theories on whether syphilis infected Columbus's crew caused its spread across Europe, see NIH, National Library of Medicine, https://pubmed.ncbi.nlm.nih.gov/24559556/. For findings that the disease existed for many hundreds of years in a mutated, nonvenereal state in the pre-Columbian new world, please see *Discover*, "The Origin of Syphilis," https://www.discovermagazine.com/health/the-origin-of-syphilis#google_vignette. See John Frith, "Syphilis—Its Early History and Treatment Until Penicillin and the Debate on Its Origins," *Journal of Military and Veterans Health* 20, no. 4 (November 2012): 49–58, https://jmvh.org/article/syphilis-its-early-history-and-treatment-until-penicillin-and-the-debate-on-its-origins/.

14. The French allege their soldiers caught syphilis from the Spaniards, who were infected by the sailors who sailed with Columbus on his first voyage. See Bullough, *History of Prostitution*, 132–34.

15. Bullough and Bullough, *Women and Prostitution*, 147–52.

16. See Holt's lye-soap making process at www.kristinholt.com.

17. Agnew, *Brides of the Multitude*, 87.

18. MacKell, *Red Light Women*, 27.

19. Deborah Hufford, "1800's Birth Control," Notes from the Frontier, https://www.notesfromthefrontier.com/post/1800s-birth-control.

20. Sheraden Seward, "The Comstock Law (1873)," Embryo Project Encyclopedia, January 13, 2009, https://embryo.asu.edu/pages/comstock-law-1873.

21. Tone, *Devices and Desires*, 53–54.

22. MacKell, *Red Light Women*, 27.

23. Frith, "Syphilis."

24. AtoZ Wiki, "Fritz Richard Schaudinn," https://atozwiki.com/Fritz_Richard_Schaudinn.

25. Kat Eschner, "The First Syphilis Cure Was the First 'Magic Bullet,'" *Smithsonian Magazine*, August 31, 2017, https://www.smithsonianmag.com/smart-news/syphilis-cure-magic-bullet-180964644/.

26. For more on penicillin, see Alina Bradford, "Penicillin: Discovery, Benefits and Resistance," Live Science, May 30, 2019, https://www.livescience.com/65598-penicillin.html.

Chapter 3

27. Hallet Stone, "Boycott of Gentile Businesses," 20–23.

28. Madsen, *Gentile Capital of Utah*, 156–77.

29. Ibid.

30. In the 1880s, the narrow-gauge Utah Northern Railway, built by Mormons, took over the northern freight traffic to serve Mormon communities. Corinne's boom went bust and its population dwindled. A twenty-five-dollar lottery ticket won the steamship *City of Corinne*. In 1878, the lack of business and other issues sealed the railway's fate: bankruptcy. The town then became an agricultural community.

31. During the nineteenth and twentieth centuries in the United States, detailed Sanborn maps were created for fire insurance companies to assess their liability in urban cities and towns. Large-scale maps depicted outlines of buildings, windows and doors, sidewalk widths and property lines, build materials, fire walls and history. Commercial Street is shown as Block 70 on one of the company's 1884 maps.

32. Whitney, *History of Utah*, 2:767–69.

33. Hampton, "Playing with Shadows," 330–440.

34. As printed in the *Mormon Expositor*, Justice Jeter Clinton, "Sermon Delivered by Dr. Jeter Clinton," 1875, picryl.com/media/mormon-expositor-salt-lake-city-utah-vol-1-no-1-1875-1.

35. Nichols, *Prostitution, Polygamy and Power*, 28–29.

36. Ibid, 29.

37. Hal Schindler, "Brigham Young's Favorite Wife," History to Go, July 30, 1995, https://historytogo.utah.gov/brigham-youngs-fav-wife/.

38. Third District Court, *Flint v. Clinton*, S9802, case 554. During the last days of the trial, Judge Emerson presided as the interim judge.

39. Nichols, *Prostitution, Polygamy and Power*, 29.

40. For more information on the propositions, see the *Deseret Evening News* from March 31, 1875.

41. *Deseret Evening News*, March 31, 1875, 52–53.

42. Find a Grave, "D. Frank Connelly," findagrave.com/memorial/40275339/d-frank-connelly.

43. *Kingdom in the West*, 13:330–440.

44. Nichols, *Prostitution, Polygamy, and Power*, 33–34.

Chapter 4

45. Alexander and Arrington, "Camp in the Sagebrush," 3–18.

46. Audrey M. Godfrey's, "Camp Floyd," History to Go, 1994, https://historytogo.utah.gov/camp-floyd/. The Mountain Meadows Massacre was the slaughter of over one hundred emigrants who were passing through Utah on their way to California. They were killed by a Mormon militia of the Nauvoo Legion, aided by uninformed (and fooled) Southern Paiute Indians.

47. Murphy, "Horn Silver Mine Crashed."

48. Gode Davis, "Frisco: The Story of Utah's Gomorrah," *Old West Magazine*, winter 1988, https://www.familysearch.org/patron/v2/TH-904-49878-533-21/dist.pdf?ctx=ArtCtxPublic.

Chapter 5

49. Harold Schindler, "The Oldest Profession's Sordid Past in Utah," stor.org/stable/j.ctt46nsdj. 53.

50. Held, *Most of John Held, Jr.*, 99–100.

Chapter 6

51. Sorenson, *Queen of the Desert*, passim.
52. Library of Congress, "Elizabeth Cady Stanton Papers: General Correspondence, 1814–1928; 1880–1884: May 21, 1880," crowd.loc. gov, transcribed and reviewed by volunteers participating in the "By the People" Project.
53. Library of Congress, National American Woman Suffrage Association Collection, https://www.nps.gov/wori/learn/historyculture/womens-suffrage-history-timeline.htm.
54. Kathy Weiser-Alexander, "Pioche, Nevada—Wildest Town in the Silver State," Legends of America, August 2022, www.LegendsofAmerica.com/Pioche-Nevada.
55. Candice Mortenson, "History," Overland Hotel & Saloon, www.overlandhotelinv.com/history/.
56. Richard E. Fike and John W. Headley, "The Pony Express Stations of Utah in Historical Perspective," Bureau of Land Management Utah, 1979, http://npshistory.com/publications/blm/cultresser/ut/2.pdf; DiCerto, *Saga of the Pony Express*, passim.
57. National Pony Express Association, www.nationalpnyexpress.org/historic-pony-express-trail/stations/.
58. National Park Service, "Historic Resources of the Tintic Mining District: Historic and Architectural Properties," https://npgallery.nps.gov/GetAsset/1e8d44b0-f62d-4f63-aebb-602984398a34.
59. Notarianni, *Faith Hope and Prosperity*, 68.
60. By 1903, the *Utah State Gazetteer and Business Directory* listed some ninety-nine businesses (establishments) in Eureka.
61. Kent Wm. Jones, "No-Nose Maggie, Juab County's Most Infamous BAD Gal of the Old West," October 17, 2020, http://nephijoneshistory.blogspot.com/2020/10/no-nose-maggie-juab-countys-most.html.
62. Benjamin H. Lehman, "Westward Ho!" November 27, 2006, https://ia800207.us.archive.org/22/items/westwardhoorvoya00kingrich/westwardhoorvoya00kingrich_djvu.txt.
63. Sorenson, *Queen of the Desert*, 52–53.
64. Ibid., 64–66.

Chapter 7

65. Richard D. Poll, "The Utah War (1815–1858)," History to Go, 1994, https://historytogo.utah.gov/utah-war/.

Chapter 8

66. Notarianni, "Helper," 153–70.

Chapter 9

67. Third District Court, criminal case no. 366, 1892; *Salt Lake Tribune*, June 23, 1892.
68. Nichols, *Prostitution, Polygamy and Power*, 100–1.
69. See June 29, 1982, *Salt Lake Tribune*.
70. Nichols, *Prostitution, Polygamy and Power*, 100–1.

Chapter 10

71. *Kingdom in the West*, 13:393–97.
72. BYU Library Special Collections, "Parsons, E.H. (Elias Howard), 1841–1920," archives.lib.byu.edu/agents/people/15092.

Chapter 11

73. In 1888, the Utah Territorial (State) Industrial School began as a juvenile reform school for both boys and girls, most sent by order of the juvenile court. In 1896, it became the Ogden Military Academy. Over the years, it faced investigations for graft, punitive punishment and deprivation. Early on, it began sending girls to the Crittenton Home.
74. J.A. Howell was the judge of the Municipal Court of Ogden City. County Attorney E.T. Hulaniski appeared as counsel for the prosecution. The defendant represented herself.

Chapter 12

75. Jeffrey D. Nichols, "Colonel Connor Filled a Varied, Dramatic Role in Utah," *History Blazer*, May 1995, https://historytogo.utah.gov/tag/colonel-connor-filled-a-varied-dramatic-role-in-utah/.

76. A notorious Union officer, Connor was known for his unrelenting massacres of Native Americans during the 1863 Indian wars in the West.

77. Captain Jim Balance, "Californians and the Military: Major General Patrick Edward Connor," California Center for Military History, State Military Reserve, militarymuseum.org/Conner.html; *Brief History of Stockton Utah* (Toole, UT: Stockton Bicentennial History Committee, 1976), http://www.stocktontown.org/stockton/site/city-history.pdf.

78. David Hampshire, Martha Sonntag Bradley and Allen Roberts, "The Settlement of Park City," in *A History of Summit County* (Salt Lake City, UT: Utah State Historical Society, 1998), 94–120.

79. Chris McLaws, "The Madam of Park City," Park City Museum, March 23, 2016, parkcityhistory.org/the madam-of-park-city/.

80. Warrens, *Park City*, passim.

81. Dalton Gackle, "Behind Closed Doors," Park City Museum, March 11, 2020, http://parkcityhistory.org/behind-closed-doors.

Chapter 13

82. Mary Smith, edited interview, 1983, Utah Marriott Library, Special Collections.

Chapter 14

83. Hallet Stone, *Hidden History of Utah*, 75–77.

84. Megan van Frank, "Fort Buenaventura: Utah's First Anglo Settlement," Utah Stories from the Beehive Archive, https://www.utahhumanities.org/stories/items/show/200.

85. *Encylopaedia Britannica*, "Al Capone," https://www.britannica.com/biography/Al-Capone.

86. See other incidents of Ogden's notorious madams in Val Holley, *25th Street Confidential* (Salt Lake City: University of Utah Press, 2013), 31–37.

87. MacKell, *Red Light Women*, 295–340.

88. Barnes, *Notorious Two-Bit Street*, 83.
89. Holley, *25ᵗʰ Street Confidential*, 38.
90. Ibid., 7, 27, 34, 39.

Chapter 15

91. Terkel, *Working*, 92.
92. McCormick, "Red Lights," 168–81.
93. As most of Salt Lake City's politics was divided along religious ideologies, the American Political Party (1904–11) was founded by mining and railroad magnate and owner of the *Salt Lake Tribune*, Senator Thomas Kearns (1901–5) and his associates who were critical of the Church of Jesus Christ of Latter-day Saints' involvement in politics.
94. Papanikolas, "Exiled Greeks," 412–30.
95. Nichols, *Prostitution, Polygamy and Power*, 142.
96. Ibid., 147.

SELECTED BIBLIOGRAPHY

Agnew, Jeremy. *Brides of the Multitude*. Lake City, CO: Western Reflections Publishing Company, 2008.

Alexander, Thomas G., and Leonard J. Arrington. "Camp in the Sagebrush: Camp Floyd, 1858–1861." *Utah Historical Quarterly* 34, no. 2 (1966): 95–120.

Alford, Kenneth, and Robert C. Freeman. "The Salt Lake Theater: Brigham's Playhouse." Brigham Young University. https://rsc.byu.edu/salt-lake-city-place-which-god-prepared/salt-lake-theatre.

Barnes, Lyle J. *Notorious Two-Bit Street*. West Conshohocken, PA: Infinity Publishing, 2009.

Bullough, Vern L. *The History of Prostitution*. New Hyde Park, NY: University Books, 1964.

Bullough, Vern, and Bonnie Bullough. *Women and Prostitution: A Social History*. Buffalo, NY: Prometheus Books, 1977.

Butler, Ann M. *Daughters of Joy, Sisters of Misery: Prostitutes in the American West, 1865–90*. Urbana: University of Illinois Press, 1985.

Campbell, Mary. *Charles Ellis Johnson and the Erotic Mormon Image*. Chicago: University of Chicago Press, 2016.

Cott, Nancy F. *History of Women in the United States: Prostitution*. Vol. 9. New Haven, CT: Yale University, 1992.

———. *History of Women in the United States: Sexuality and Sexual Behavior*. Vol. 10. New Haven, CT: Yale University, 1993.

Davis, Daniel. "Appreciating a Pretty Shoulder: The Risquie Images of Charles Ellis Johnson." *Utah Historical Quarterly* 74, no. 2 (2006): 131–46.

DiCerto, Joseph J. *The Saga of the Pony Express*. Missoula, MT: Mountain Press Publishing Co., 2002.

Hallet Stone, Eileen. "Boycott of Gentile Businesses Couldn't Outlast Progress." In *Hidden History of Utah*. Charleston, SC: The History Press, 2013.

Hampton, Brigham Young. "Playing with Shadows, Voices of Dissent." In *Kingdom in the West: The Mormons and the American Frontier*. Vol. 13. Norman, OK: Arthur H. Clark Co., 2011.

Held, John. *The Most of John Held, Jr*. Brattleboro, VT: Stephen Green Press, 1972.

Holley, Val. *25th Street Confidential*. Salt Lake City: University of Utah Press, 2013.

MacKell, Jan. *Red Light Women of the Rocky Mountains*. Albuquerque: University of New Mexico Press, 2009.

Madsen, Brigham H. *The Gentile Capital of Utah*. Salt Lake City: Utah Historical Society, 1980.

McCormick, John S. "Red Lights in Zion." *Utah Historical Quarterly* 50, no. 2 (1982): 168–81.

Murphy, Miriam B. "When the Horn Silver Mine Crashed In." History to Go. https://historytogo.utah.gov/horn-silver-mine.

Nichols, Jeffrey. *Prostitution, Polygamy and Power*. Urbana: University of Illinois Press, 2002.

Notarianni, Philip F. *Faith, Hope and Prosperity: The Tintic Mining District*. Eureka, UT: Tintic Historical Society, 1982.

———. "Helper—The Making of a Gentile Town in Zion." In *Carbon County, Eastern Utah's Industrialized Island*. Salt Lake City: Utah Historical Society, 1981.

Papanikolas, Helen Z. "The Exiled Greeks." In *The Peoples of Utah*. Edited by Helen Z. Papanikolas. Salt Lake City, UT: Salt Lake Historical Society, 1976.

Rosen, Ruth. *The Lost Sisterhood: Prostitution in America: 1900–1918*. Baltimore, MD: Johns Hopkins University Press, 1982.

Rutter, Michael. *Upstairs Girls: Prostitution in the American West*. Helena, MT: FairCountry Press, 2005.

Seagraves, Anne. *Soiled Doves: Prostitution in the Early West*. Hayden, ID: Wesanne Publication, 1994.

Sorenson, Jody Tesch. *Queen of the Desert: The Real Story of Mary Devitt Laird.* Madison: Wisconsin Historical Society, 2007.

Terkel, Studs. *Working.* New York: Avon Books, 1975.

Tone, Andrea. *Devices and Desires.* New York: Hill and Wang, 2001.

Warrens, Larry. *Park City: Mountain of Treasure.* Missoula, MT: Mountain Press Publishing Co., 2004.

Whitney, Orson F. *History of Utah.* Vol 2. Salt Lake City, UT: George Q. Cannon & Sons, 1893.

INDEX

ABOUT THE AUTHOR

*T*ransplanted from New England, Utah-based writer Eileen Hallet Stone's projects include issues of equity, community stories, ethnic histories and more about people and their work and lifestyle. She has written extensively for Utah magazines and newspapers and teaches for the OSHER Lifelong Learning Institute at the University of Utah. In 1996, she coauthored *Missing Stories: An Oral History of Ethnic and Minority Groups in Utah* (1996), which has been used extensively by Utah educators to diversify their curriculum. Her collected stories in *A Homeland in the West: Utah Jews Remember* were developed into a photograph documentary exhibit for the 2002 Winter Olympic Cultural Olympiad Arts Festival in Salt Lake City. Her commentaries are featured in the 2015 documentary film *Carvalho's Journey*; KUED's 2016 PBS documentary, *Pioneer Diaries*; and the January 2017 KUED series, *Utah Conversations with Ted Capener*. Her books, which include *Hidden History of Utah* (2013*)*, *Historic Tales of Utah* (2016) and *Auerbach's: The Store that Performs What it Promises* (2018), began with compilations from the "Living History" column she wrote for the *Salt Lake Tribune*. She lives with her librarian husband, Randy Silverman, in the lively Sugar House area of Salt Lake City.